To Peter,

Fantastic to meet
you, hope the
show & book provides
inspiration!

Best

Forgotten Spirits & Long Lost Liqueurs

by David T. Smith

Published by White Mule Press,
a division of the American Distilling Institute™

© 2015 White Mule Press

Printed in the United States of America.

ISBN 978-0-9910436-6-8

whitemulepress.com
cheers@whitemulepress.com

PO Box 577
Hayward, CA 94541
USA

Illustrations © Sara L. Smith

CONTENTS

PREFACE

Jerry Thomas wrote, what is believed to be, one of the first books of cocktail recipes in 1862. By the end of the nineteenth century there were at least a dozen more that preserved many of today's great cocktails. Classic drinks such as the Martini and the Manhattan only make up a small minority of the drinks included in their pages. So what about the others?

Some of these vintage cocktails fell from grace due to changes in public taste, but others disappeared simply because you could not make them anymore. Throughout the first quarter of the twentieth century, many of the key spirits, bitters, and liqueurs used to create these early drinks were no longer produced. An Aviation without crème de violette, a Moulin Rouge without orange gin, or a Tom Collins without Old Tom gin became poor reflections of their former selves.

This book investigates the origins and histories of these forgotten spirits, bitters and long-lost liqueurs. The book also explores some new iterations of these ingredients that have been resurrected or recreated for the first time in a century. For those ingredients that still do not have any commercially available brands, the book includes simple recipes that can be used by the reader to recreate them. These recipes can be found in the appendix along with a large collection of vintage cocktail recipes.

One such ingredient that was lost, in fact banned, from the US and has now returned, is absinthe. However, it will not be covered in this book, as a mere chapter would not do justice to a subject worthy of its own volume. Those interested in the topic can find some suggested reading in the back.

Lastly, this book builds upon some of the excellent and passionate work from a collection of cocktail archaeologists. Their work has been an inspiration, but special mention goes to Ted Haigh, aka Dr. Cocktail, who has done a great amount to encourage research in this area.

OLD TOM GIN

Old Tom gin is the preeminent long-lost spirit: it was one of the most popular ingredients used in the recipe books from the Golden Era of cocktails, and there are a growing number of Old Tom Gins now on the market. The revival of Old Tom is the most successful in the world of lost spirits.

HISTORY

During the "Gin Craze" of the eighteenth century, gin in Great Britain was not a spirit of the standard and quality that we have and expect today. The underlying alcohol was frequently unrefined and, all too often, cut with noxious substances. In order to make this questionable liquor more palatable, the spirit was infused with herbs and spices to mask the poor flavor and sweetened, often with sugar, to remove some of the burn. This style of gin became known as "Old Tom" gin.

The exact origins of the term "Old Tom" are those of myth and legend, but one often cited theory dates from the Gin Acts of the 1730s, which cracked down on the illegal distilling that plagued London. In his autobiographical book, *Life and Unusual Adventures of Captain Dudley Bradstreet* (1755), Captain Bradstreet recalled:

> The Mob being very noisy and clamorous for want of their beloved Liquor, which few or none at last dared to sell, it soon occurred to me to venture upon that Trade. I bought the Act, and read it over several times, and found no Authority by it to break open Doors, and that the Informer must know the Name of the Person who rented the House it was sold in. To evade this, I got an Acquaintance to take a House in Blue Anchor Alley in St. Luke's Parish, who privately convey'd his Bargain to me; I then got it well secured, and laid out in a Bed and other Furniture five Pounds, in Provision and Drink that would keep about two Pounds, and purchased in Moorfields the Sign of a Cat, and had it nailed to a Street Window; I then caused a Leaden Pipe, the small End out about an Inch, to be placed under the Paw of the Cat; the End that was within had a Funnel to it.

> When my House was ready for Business, I enquired [sic] what Distiller in London was most famous for good Gin, and was assured by several, that it was Mr. L-dale in Holbourn: To him I went and laid out thirteen Pounds, which was all the Money I had, except two Shillings, and told him my Scheme, which he approved of. This Cargo was sent

off to my House, at the Back of which there was a Way to go in or out. When the Liquor was properly disposed, I got a Person to inform a few of the Mob, that Gin would be sold by the Cat at my Window next Day, provided they put the Money in its Mouth, from whence there was a Hole that conveyed it to me. At Night I took Possession of my Den, and got up early next Morning to be ready for Custom; it was near three Hours before any body called, which made me almost despair of the Project; at last I heard the Chink of Money, and a comfortable Voice say, "Puss, give me two Pennyworth of Gin." I instantly put my Mouth to the Tube, and bid them receive it from the Pipe under her Paw, and then measured and poured it into the Funnel, from whence they soon received it.

Whilst this story illustrates a connection between gin and cats, it is conspicuous for its lack of mentioning the term in question "Old Tom."

A more likely theory for how Old Tom got its name is alluded to in the legal case Boord & Son vs. Huddart from 1903. The court records show that the plaintiff, Boord, had registered the cat and barrel brand in 1879, but had been using it since September 28, 1849. Boord had marked this date in a ledger as "the first printing of the 'Cat and Barrel' label." Huddart, the defendant, had been using the cat and barrel logo on a bottle of sloe gin that they produced.

Boord & Sons also "established that they were the first people to connect the words 'Old Tom' with a cat." and were recorded as being "ridiculed at the time for adopting the cat on a barrel." However, they adopted the cat mark because of a legend that a cat had once fallen into one of their gin vats.

The court records revealed a few interesting facts. First, the document continuously referred to Old Tom as a "sweetened" gin. This is noteworthy because a number of writers have perpetuated the myth, first printed in the 1910 *Encyclopædia Britannica*, that a court case established that Old Tom was originally unsweetened. Second, the court stated, "the precise origin of the term Old Tom as applied to sweetened gin [was] 'lost in obscurity.'" And third, that one of the earliest references to Old Tom gin was by Boz (Charles Dickens) in a piece published in the Evening Chronicle from February 19, 1835. Dickens described the gin shop as having "two side-aisles of great casks, painted green and gold, enclosed within a light brass rail and bearing such inscriptions, as 'Old Tom, 549;' 'Young Tom, 360;' 'Samson, 1421'–the figures agreeing, we presume, with 'gallons', understood."

The case also mentions that early gin labels depicted (old) Tom as a human, who may have been Thomas Chamberlain of Hodges' Distillery. This distillery, in Lambeth, London, which has long since closed down, at one time boasted its own fire brigade, in part, to protect itself from the surrounding fire hazards, including fireworks, tallow, and candleworks factories. There are also tales of a brand labeled Young Tom Gin, which had a sailor on the bottle, although evidence of this is thin. Further support to the idea that "Tom" refers to a person and not a feline comes in the form of old gin bottles embossed with "Old Uncle Tom Gin. "

Booth's, founded in the 1740s, was the first of the reputable eighteenth century gin houses. The introduction of the column still, continuous distillation and other developments in distillation methods, greatly improved the quality of spirits produced. As a result, the need to disguise unpleasant flavors lessened and sweetened gin became a matter of taste.

Over the next century, gin houses launched more brands, all with a greater focus on their reputation and quality control. Almost all of the big gin houses produced an Old Tom and brands such as Tanqueray offered both sweetened and unsweetened versions of their gin. At the same time, a dryer style of gin became more popular. Public taste continued to evolve towards unsweetened gins and increasingly dry Martinis, especially after the Second World War. Gordon's, the last of the British distillers to make an Old Tom gin, discontinued theirs in the 1960s.

Old Tom gin and the cocktails that called for it fell into obscurity until the beginning of the twenty-first century. In 2007, Hayman's Distillers, a family firm descended from James Burrough, founder of Beefeater Gin, released an Old Tom gin based on a recipe from the 1860s. This was the first Old Tom gin produced in Britain in over 40 years.

THE FLAVOR OF OLD TOM GIN

Today, there are more than a dozen Old Tom gins available worldwide, each of which fits into one of four categories: sugar-sweetened, botanically sweetened, American style ould tom, and in name only. With all of these modern interpretations, it is worth remembering that the reason for the existence of the Old Tom style was to cover the unpleasant flavors of the underlying alcohol. With modern distillation techniques and quality control, this is no longer an issue and no modern distiller would want to use inferior ingredients. One theory of how to compensate for this was suggested a few years ago by distiller Charles Maxwell: by adding some new-make whisky spirit to gin, one can simulate the more characterful base of early Old Toms without reducing the quality of the product.

SUGAR SWEETENED

This style of Old Tom gin is typically sweetened with cane sugar and was often, but not always, more botanically intense than a modern dry gin. This was the style adopted by most of the big gin houses over 100 years ago. Gordon's Old Tom gin is described in an advert from the 1930s as "Gordon's Dry Gin with Real Cane Sugar." Two historical recipes found in the archives at Beefeater, one for a dry gin and another for an Old Tom, have identical methods and botanical mixes, with the only difference being that the Old Tom recipe calls for 40lbs of sugar for every 100 gallons of liquid. Below are a few contemporary expressions of sugar-sweetened Old Tom gin.

BOTH'S OLD TOM GIN (47.0% ABV)

Both's Distillery, founded in 1886, currently makes their Old Tom Gin for Haromex of Germany. Both's designed it to reflect the Old Tom gins of the nineteenth century, for use in cocktails such as the Martinez.

NOSE: Bold citrus lemon with herbal undertones.

TASTE: Sweet citrus and juniper, along with fennel anise, reminiscent of the herbal liqueurs of the European mountains. This has a silky texture and the gin is pleasant to drink neat, although, at 47% ABV, it is certainly powerful for an Old Tom.

THE DORCHESTER OLD TOM GIN 2007 (40.0% ABV)

William Grant & Sons, the folks behind Hendrick's Gin, made this exclusively for The Dorchester Hotel in London. They created it so the barmen there could authentically recreate some of the truly classic cocktails.

NOSE: Delicate and fragrant, with hints of rose and sandalwood; undoubtedly perfume-like.

TASTE: Sweet, but not without dryness, this gin also has some floral notes. It is silky and smooth with hints of lavender and violet, whilst also being reminiscent of a coniferous forest. Very good and well balanced, with a real depth of character.

As of 2014, City of London Distillers produces The Dorchester Old Tom gin.

GOLDENCOCK GIN (38.0% ABV)

Dating from the late 1920s and made in Norway by Arcus, Gold-

encock is the only Old Tom gin that remained in production while all others disappeared. Given that it is not exported from Norway, it remained largely unknown for decades, with only scant reference in a few books. The gin is sweetened with cane, botanically intense and has a little aged spirit added to provide a richer texture.

NOSE: Juniper, coriander, citrus sweetness.

TASTE: Strong and intense flavor with herbal notes upfront; rosemary thyme and a hint of mint followed by some juniper pine. This is followed by a little sweet spice, lots of licorice and then a dry citrus finish.

HAMMER & SONS OLD ENGLISH GIN (44.0% ABV)

Hammer & Sons Old English Gin is made at the Langley distillery in the oldest gin still in the UK, with a recipe dating from 1783. The gin contains a mix of 11 botanicals (juniper, coriander, angelica, lemon, orange, orris root, cardamom, cassia, licorice, cinnamon, and nutmeg) and 4 grams of sugar per liter. The gin is unusually packaged in reused champagne bottles with a silkscreen print.

NOSE: Vibrant, sweet lemon and vanilla, like lemon cheesecake, with a little soapy coriander, before returning to a fresher, lemon note.

TASTE: Very smooth, with a hint of sweetness to start that is quickly outshone by strong notes of juniper, lemongrass, and coriander. The finish is of soapy coriander, juniper, and a dry note like wood crossed with soda water.

HAYMAN'S OLD TOM GIN (40.0% ABV)

This was the first of the new recreations of Old Tom gin. It is lightly sweetened and botanically intense, and is based on a historical recipe from James Burrough, the ancestor of Hayman's current Master Distiller, Christopher Hayman.

NOSE: A good, solid juniper nose, plus a little sweet citrus, like orange cremes.

TASTE: Very clearly gin, with a slightly more intense flavor and an added sweetness. This is a neat product that is quite easy to drink. If you see Old Tom as sweetened gin with a little more bang from the botanicals, this would be a good choice.

PROFESSOR CORNELIUS AMPLEFORTH'S OLD TOM GIN (42.4% ABV)

This gin was originally created as an ingredient for The Handmade Cocktail Company's bottled Martinez Cocktail. Botanically intense, it is sweetened with a little sugar.

NOSE: Juniper and spice.

TASTE: Sweet upfront with a flash of juniper and then plenty of spice such as cinnamon, nutmeg, cassia, cloves and vanilla, followed by some orange and then a sugar-sweet finish. Big, bold, sweet and spicy.

QUEEN'S COURAGE NEW YORK OLD TOM GIN (45.0% ABV)

Launched in June 2014 after years of research, the Astoria Distilling Company makes Queen's Courage in New York. They produce this gin using a combination of neutral and malt spirit. The malt spirit is not only a nod to New York's Dutch history, but also adds more character and a richer mouthfeel. The collection of six gin botanicals is distilled in three separate batches to maintain a greater harmony of flavors. White grapefruit adds a fragrant bitterness that is neatly balanced out by the sweetness of New York honey, sourced, in part, from Queens.

COLOR: Very light straw.

NOSE: Soft, sweet grain with a hint of cardamom spice, before notes of cocoa paste, buttery biscuit, and vanilla, then a lighter, fruity note at the end: spiced grape and dried apple. A vermouth-like grapefruit citrus aroma adds a slightly sour note towards the end. After a while, there are even notes of plump cherry fruit and stones, followed by bright zesty citrus.

TASTE: A rich spirit with an initial silky and viscous texture, followed by warmth. There is plenty of spice, such as nutmeg, grains of paradise, menthol, pepper, and black cardamom. This is followed by bright zesty citrus, which has a hint of dry bitterness. Finally, a mix of cherry and apricot notes, with just a touch of grape on the finish.

TANQUERAY OLD TOM GIN (47.3% ABV)

Released in 2014, 93 years after the originally Tanqueray Old Tom was discontinued. The gin uses the classic four Tanqueray botanicals (juniper, coriander, angelica and licorice) but in a greater quantity to the original, making it more botanically intense. After distillation, some new-make wheat spirit is added. This new-make wheat spirit is usually aged for use in Johnnie Walker Blended Scotch. Finally, the gin is sweetened with some beet sugar.

NOSE: Juniper and coriander, supported by a light but creamy citrus note, reminiscent of a lemon cheesecake; a touch of black pepper towards the end.

TASTE: A very powerful spirit with an intense flavor profile; heaps of juniper and coriander and some dryness from the angelica. Then, a rich complexity from the new-make base comes through, adding some spice and other bready notes, followed by a light sweetness. The finish is fresh and juicy with fruit and then a touch of fresh black pepper.

BOTANICALLY~SWEETENED

In this style, no sugar is added at all; instead, the sweetness comes from the botanicals, typically licorice. This is based on the historical practice of finding other ways to sweeten spirits, thereby avoiding the extra expense of buying sugar. Below are a few contemporary expressions of botanically-sweetened Old Tom gin.

JENSEN'S OLD TOM GIN (43.0% ABV)

From the creator of the Bermondsey Gin, this Old Tom is based on an original recipe dating back to the 1840s. While Jensen takes the view that Old Tom gin was historically sweetened in order to hide impurities in the gin, the sweetness in his recipe comes from a more intense botanical mix because, he suggests, the cost of sugar in 1840 was prohibitively high.

NOSE: Juniper and heavy spice on the nose, with a hint of resin. This is complex, with quite a bit of depth.

TASTE: Not overly sweet. A lot of the elements from the nose come out on the taste: pine and strong herbal elements. The finish is reminiscent of licorice powder, and this is where any sweetness comes from. Definitely distinctive from any other Old Tom gin currently available.

SECRET TREASURES 2007 (40.0% ABV)

This is part of Haromex's Secret Treasures Collection from Germany and was created by Master Blender, Hubertus Vallendar, in Kail. Only 688 bottles were produced in 2007. It used a double distillation process and the juniper comes from Italy's Apennine Mountains.

NOSE: Soft, with juniper and floral notes and then some sweet elements.

TASTE: A very fresh beginning, like cucumber, the skin in particular. There's a hint of sweetness, but the gin remains quite dry overall. Notes of pine and a little oak appear at the end. This is dryer than most Old Tom gins, but the sweeter character is certainly there.

AMERICAN STYLE OULD TOM GIN

A style popularized by American craft distillers, ould tom gin is a hybrid of geneva and gin, that is sometimes sweetened. It is also common for it to be aged for a few months in wood. There are a growing number of American-style Ould Tom Gins in the market. Below are a few expressions currently available.

CORSAIR MAJOR TOM (44.0%ABV)

This gin uses the same botanical mix as Corsair's original gin; the finished product is then lightly aged in wood. After aging, the gin is infused with additional botanicals and spices, and is sweetened with Tupelo honey.

COLOR: Light amber-brown.

NOSE: Stalky green notes, reminiscent of spiced cabbage, drawn together with lots of eucalyptus and a little vanilla; fresh mint towards the end.

TASTE: A very sugary sweet start, followed by intense herbal notes and a strong, underlying note of peppery celery. After a while, spiced notes of hot cinnamon also come through. The finish has notes of chocolate, light vanilla, and more vegetal elements. More celery at the end, combined with a hint of sweetness, before a dry mouthfeel.

DOWNSLOPE OULD TOM GIN (42.5 %ABV)

Made by Downslope Distillers near Denver, Colorado, it is designed as an interpretation of a late 1800s-style gin. It contains a mix of

seven botanicals and is aged in wood for a number of months.
COLOR: Golden orange.
NOSE: Some dry cider apple notes and then some bready maltiness.
TASTE: A good full texture with some ripe apple to start, followed by some sweet herbal notes, cinnamon and nutmeg. Reminiscent of a spiced baked apple. This is followed by a little maltiness and then some dry citrus, juniper and a hint of chocolate. A very complex example of ould tom gin, and as sippable as a malt whisky.

LANGHAM OLD TOM GIN (42.0% ABV)

Made especially for the Artisan Bar at the Langham Hotel, this is a blend of two mystery gins and some nuts, which is then aged in a barrel.
NOSE: Engaging with notes of tea, toffee, dark chocolate and bran flakes.
TASTE: Very complex. A bittersweet start is followed by a dryness, followed by sweet nuttiness such as hazelnut and just a hint of walnut. The finish is reminiscent of tannins; such as you might get from a tea liqueur.

RANSOM OLD TOM GIN (44.0% ABV)

Released in 2009, Ransom was designed to be a recreation of the type of gin consumed in the US at the end of the nineteenth century. It is made in Sheridan, Oregon, with a base spirit of malted barley and high-strength corn spirit. The gin is then aged in Pinot Noir barrels.
COLOR: Medium orange-brown.
NOSE: Pine, sap, a hint of cedar wood and cardamom.
TASTE: There was a little smooth silkiness at the start, followed by sappy, piney juniper, some vanilla and oak. There were herbal hints, too, and a little warmth towards the end. The wood then comes through again with a flavor that is very much like freshly cut wood: natural and forest-like.

SOUNDS SPIRITS OLD TOM GIN (40.0% ABV)

Made by Sound Spirits of Seattle, Washington, which holds the moniker of being Seattle's first distillery since prohibition. Their Old Tom gin is rested on oak chips for about a month; it uses less juniper and more spice than the distillery's Ebb and Flow dry gin.
COLOR: Very light yellow.
NOSE: Warm citrus, lemon, lime and orange, with complex spiced notes.
TASTE: A good spiciness up front of nutmeg, cinnamon and ginger, followed by some citrus and juniper, then coriander and finally some dry floral notes on a long finish.

SPRING 44 (44.0% ABV)

Made in Loveland, Colorado, this Old Tom gin contains a mix of 7 botanicals: juniper, coriander seed, orris root, lemongrass, rosemary, galangal root and pink grapefruit peel. The gin is aged in new–toasted–not charred, American oak barrels for 6 months, to add a little warmth.

NOSE: Very strong piney juniper, but with an intriguing vegetal note alongside it and some sweetness, too, like celery with hints of sweet licorice powder.

TASTE: The same vegetal notes from the nose come through on the taste, with a combination of savory, sour and bitter notes, including celery. The finish is slightly sweet, like licorice sticks, with more straightforward notes of piney juniper at the very end.

VALENTINE LIBERATOR OLD TOM GIN (45.2% ABV)

Based on the original Liberator Gin, but with a slight tweak to the original mix of nine botanicals to give greater emphasis on some of the sweeter spices. This Old Tom gin is aged in American oak for two years.

COLOR: Warm gold.

NOSE: Complex and aromatic, with cinnamon, a hint of cardamom, and a touch of vanilla oak.

TASTE: Spicy and complex with a rich mouthfeel and a little sweetness. Strong, spiced notes of cinnamon and cardamom, as well as some light, floral elements. Vanilla and wood then make way for dry juniper and a little black pepper and menthol on the finish.

IN NAME ONLY

This final style refers to two gins that feature the words "Old Tom" on their labels, but not as a reflection of the style of the gin in the bottle, a fact that the author can confirm, having tried both. These include Wray & Nephews Old Tom Gin from Jamaica and the twenty-first century incarnation of Boord's made in Missouri.

COCKTAILS

Martinez

The classic Old Tom drink is a variation on the early Manhattan. Recipes can be found in the Modern Bartender's Guide by O. H. Byron (1884) and in Jerry Thomas' 1887 Bartenders Guide, which simply described it as a "Manhattan but with gin replacing whisky." Unlike modern Martinis, the Martinez has a higher proportion of vermouth to gin. This works because the added botanical intensity of Old Tom gins can stand up to the flavors of the vermouth. The extra sweetness in the gin also helps to balance the bitter finish of the wormwood, which is especially apparent if you use a vermouth-like Carpano Antica Formula.

4 parts red vermouth
2 parts Old Tom gin
2 dashes maraschino
2 dashes Boker's bitters
Stir

Tom Collins

This recipe is adapted from Barflies and Cocktails by Harry & Wynn. Using Old Tom rather than dry gin adds a smoother texture to the drink and increases the flavor of juniper and other botanicals. Using an American style of ould tom gin adds a rich complexity with oak, spice and some malty notes.

3 parts Old Tom gin
3 parts lemon juice
6 parts club soda
1 tsp sugar

These are just two iconic cocktails that call for Old Tom gin and illustrate the difference it makes to a drink.

Navy Gin

The expanse of the British Empire was only possible due to the Royal Navy, which connected the various colonies and territories. And, whilst an army is said to "march on its stomach," another supply was equally essential to naval crews and officers: their spirits ration. The spirits ration, replacing a previous ration of beer, was introduced in 1655. Able seamen were typically given rum, whilst officers drank gin. However, beer, wine, port, arrack, or any other liquor that could be picked up from a local ports on a ship's voyage, were also known to have been consumed.

In the early days of distilling there was no precise way to measure the alcoholic strength of a distilled spirit; therefore, mixing a pinch of gunpowder with the spirit and then igniting it determined the alcohol content. If the powder lit with a steady flame, then the spirit was "proof;" this strength became known as 100 English Proof. Later, 100 proof was calculated to be 57.15% alcohol by volume (ABV). It is worth noting that the English Proof system differs from the American one, the latter being simply double the ABV.

There are a couple of theories as to why navy gins are 57% ABV. An often cited idea is that any gunpowder that had gin spilt on it would still ignite if that gin was at 100 British proof; however, most British warships from the nineteenth century had a separate powder magazine and spirits room, making this an unlikely explanation. More plausible is that, as the spirit was often mixed and diluted for consumption, a higher strength gin would go further, making more drinks and a more efficient use of the limited space on ship. An even higher alcoholic strength would be more efficient still; but, above 57% ABV, the spirit would become less stable and more flammable.

Naval officers' fondness for gin helps to explain why eighteenth century distillers were thriving in the naval towns of Portsmouth, Plymouth, Bristol and Deptford. The incoming spice traders to these ports also provided a plentiful supply of the fresh botanicals used in gin. The Blackfriars Distillery in Plymouth started making their navy-strength gin in the 1850s. By 1855, they were annually shipping around 1,000 barrels, the modern equivalent of 23,000 cases, to the Royal Navy. This spirit, bottled at 100 English Proof (57% ABV), became the gin of choice for such drinks as the Pink Gin and Gimlet.

For over a century and a half, Blackfriars Distillery continued to make their 100 proof gin by special request from the Royal Navy. This special edition gin was essentially their regular gin with less water dilution. Between 1863 and 1950, Burrough's Distillery in London made a Senior Service, (a synonym for the Royal Navy) gin for the ships based at the Royal Dock at Deptford, London.

Until 2011, navy gin had limited availability to the public in the UK and almost no availability outside the UK. During their bicentennial in 1993, Blackfriars Distillery's made their 100 proof gin a permanent fixture in their product portfolio, although the name was formally changed to "Navy Strength." For the next 18 years, Plymouth Navy Strength Gin was only available at selected outlets in the UK, despite demand from bartenders in the US. Then, in 2011, new distillers formulated and released their own navy gins to meet the US market demand. Leopolds, in the Fall/

Autumn 2011, was first to the release, followed by Hayman's Royal Dock (2012), New York Distilling's Perry's Tot (2012), FEW Standard Issue (2012), Professor Cornelius Ampleforth (2012), Hernö (2013), Sipsmith (2013) and Genius (2014).

Today, navy gin is understood as any gin bottled at 100 English Proof (57-58% ABV). In contrast, a gin bottled at 56% ABV is "under proof" and one bottled at over 58% ABV is "over proof." Neither is technically navy gin.

THE FLAVOR OF NAVY GIN

Today, navy gins fall into two categories of production: Original Botanical Mix, and Modified Botanical Mix. Original Botanical Mix navy gins are higher strength versions of the distillers' original gins, i.e. less dilute. The differences in taste are due to both the higher alcohol content and the fact that the botanical oils are more concentrated and thus the aromas and flavors are more intense at a higher ABV. Modified Botanical Mix navy gins have different or modified recipes from the original gin. Differences might include increasing the juniper or the general botanical intensity so that the gin is bolder in terms of both alcohol and flavor.

ORIGINAL BOTANICAL MIX

HERNÖ NAVY (57.0%ABV)

This is a higher strength version of the Hernö Swedish Excellence Gin. Distilled at the world's northernmost distillery in Angermanland, Sweden, it is made using a mix of eight botanicals, including meadowsweet, vanilla, lingonberries and black peppercorns.

NOSE: Sappy pine and juniper notes, coriander and a hint of beeswax and citrus—very intense.

TASTE: Silky smooth to start, with plenty of spice and citrus coriander. There is then a little warmth with some sweetness and notes of juniper. The coriander then returns with citrus, and a crisp and long-lasting finish that lasts for well over 90 seconds. Flavorful and intense, it really shows how the higher ABV carries the botanical characteristics in a far bolder way.

GENIUS GIN NAVY STRENGTH (57.0% ABV)

Made by Genius Liquids from Austin, Texas. The gin is simply a higher ABV version of the standard gin and the botanicals are distilled using a combination of 72-hour macerated pot distillation and vapor infusion.

NOSE: Clean, with a touch of sweetness that comes from the can base spirit; it is almost reminiscent of a white rum. There is also a little creamy spice, followed by dry citrus.

TASTE: A full flavor with a rich mouthfeel. Initially, there's a thick, creamy sweetness, which moves to some of the more traditional gin flavors: juniper, angelica and coriander. There is then a touch of spice, before a powerful, long and lingering, dry finish.

PLYMOUTH NAVY STRENGTH (57.0% ABV)

Plymouth Navy Strength is a higher strength version of their standard gin or, simply put, "Their 41.2% ABV gin, but with less water."

NOSE: Juniper upfront, followed by citrus, coriander, earthy notes and a touch of cardamom.

TASTE: A strong and intense flavor, almost a little peppery. The style is very classic, with piney juniper, fresh and zingy citrus, and a slight sweetness towards the end, which is slightly reminiscent of caramelized orange peel.

ROYAL DOCK NAVY STRENGTH GIN (57.0% ABV)

Based on a recipe from 1863, Royal Dock is made by the Hayman family at their distillery in Witham, UK, using neutral grain spirit and a blend of nine classic gin botanicals.

NOSE: Classic and fresh, with juniper, citrus and licorice.

TASTE: Again, this is a very classic style of gin and is smooth, clean and crisp. There is a good dose of juniper, which is refreshed by the citrus peel, coriander and spicy herbal notes–an excellent example of a navy gin: strong, yet smooth.

MODIFIED BOTANICAL MIX

FEW STANDARD ISSUE (57.0% ABV)

Made by FEW Spirits, a distillery in Evanston, Illinois, their Standard Issue gin uses a different spirit base and botanical mix compared to their American Gin. It has a greater focus on the more intense botanical flavors of juniper and fennel.

NOSE: Fragrant, with piney juniper, coriander, and some more flowery notes. There is also a faint, crisp, vegetal quality reminiscent of a freshly picked tomato.

TASTE: Very flavorful with some maltiness and creaminess. Coriander and floral notes, such as honeysuckle, are followed by a leafy herbal flavor and sweet pepper toward the end.

LEOPOLD'S NAVY STRENGTH (57.0% ABV)

This is more botanically intense than Leopold's American Gin and is made using bergamot rather than pomelo. Like the original gin, each botanical is distilled separately and then blended together.

NOSE: Strong, piney juniper; bold and intense.

TASTE: Sweet and very heavy on the pine, this has plenty of herbal notes. It is very warming, with a warmth that gradually builds over time. The intensity in the gin is reflected by both the ABV and the flavors of the botanicals, making this a gin that will stand up to mixing in most gin cocktails.

NEW YORK DISTILLING PERRY'S TOT NAVY STRENGTH GIN (57.0% ABV)

Made by New York Distilling, based in Brooklyn, New York, using a mix of ten botanicals, including cinnamon, cardamom and star anise. It is named after Matthew Calbraith Perry, who served as Commandant of the Brooklyn Navy Yard from 1841-43.

NOSE: Complex, with overriding characteristics of pine and coriander, as well as some other, deeper herbal notes.

TASTE: A more contemporary style of gin, with an immediate burst of flavor that's invigorating and exciting. Strong citrus and coriander followed by sweet licorice root.

PROFESSOR CORNELIUS AMPLEFORTH'S BATHTUB GIN NAVY STRENGTH (57.0% ABV)

A stronger version of the Professor's Bathtub Gin, made by infusing crushed, rather than whole, botanicals in spirit, thus increasing the gin's botanical intensity.

NOSE: Juniper, cinnamon and nutmeg.

TASTE: Soft to start, followed by a huge burst of flavor: cinnamon, coriander, nutmeg and cloves. Rather Christmassy, with a fair amount of warmth, but not burn, from the alcohol. This is a good choice for seasonal cocktails around the festive period; it'll really warm the cockles.

SIPSMITH V.J.O.P. #3 (57.7% ABV)

Sipsmith Very Juniper Over Proof (VJOP) #3 is the British version of a gin previously made exclusively for the Japanese market. It is made using the same ten botanicals as the original Sipsmith Gin, plus additional juniper. The other botanicals have a mix of maceration time and some are even vapor-infused, which is distinctly different to the standard maceration method used for their classic gin. For the British version, the ABV was increased from 52% ABV and thus, it can be considered a navy gin.

NOSE: Big and bold, with strong juniper, floral citrus and coriander.

TASTE: Remarkably smooth and sippable, especially given the alcoholic strength; the warmth only really comes through right at the end. There are flavors of crisp juniper, spicy coriander, citrus, and a hint of fresh black pepper.

3 HOWLS NAVY STRENGTH GIN (57.0% ABV)

Distilled in Seattle, Washington at the 3 Howls Distillery, this gin is produced using a combination of pot and vapor infusion distillation. This process leaves some residual color in the spirit.

COLOR: Light straw.

NOSE: Juniper and coriander, with hints of salt and zest.

TASTE: Lots of juniper upfront, followed by a flash of vanilla and then some spiced flavors such as nutmeg, cinnamon, ginger and cardamom. Towards the end, there is dry angelica and a little salt. Complex, but interesting and very easy to sip; particularly smooth for 57.0% ABV.

COCKTAILS

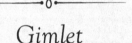

Pink Gin

A Pink Gin is a traditional naval cocktail that mixed gin and Angostura Bitters. Once considered a cure for seasickness, these bitters are made by the House of Angostura in Trinidad and Tobago, a former British Colony. Angostura turns gin pink, while its herbs and spices complement the botanicals of gin.

4 parts navy gin
4-5 dashes Angostura bitters
Stir

Gimlet

This cocktail derives its name from two possible sources: it is either named after a tool used to bore holes or, after Royal Navy surgeon, Sir Thomas Gimlette. The drink contains lime juice, which was used to help prevent scurvy on long sea voyages. It is possible that the navy used limes because they were easy to come by in the British colonies, even though lemons actually contain more vitamin C.

Some traditionalists insist on the use of Rose's Lime Cordial for their Gimlet, while others prefer to make their own. This can be done by mixing a 2:1 ratio of lime juice to sugar and adding a little vodka so that it will keep longer.

4 parts navy gin
2 parts lime cordial
Shake

In addition, navy gin works well as a pre-dinner Martini or in a Gin & Tonic.

Yellow Gin

Spirits have been stored in wood since the fifteenth century. In addition to providing a useful method of storage, wooden casks interact with their contents and impart, in varying degrees, some of their character on the spirit's flavor. In the seventeenth and eighteenth centuries, spirits were sold to patrons in the public houses of the day, and directly from the cask. Some landlords would even blend their own spirits and wines into casks on site; such was the norm in the grand Victorian gin palaces of Britain. It is important to note that the impact of the wood on the gin was, at that time, incidental. Little attention was given to the woods used in the barrels. In addition, barrels would be constantly used and reused, as long as they were structurally sound. Also, it would have been common for gin barrels to have previously held something else.

During the nineteenth century there were significant changes in how gin was produced and consumed. The quality of gin drastically improved with the founding of the great gin houses: Booth's, Dakin, Gordon's, Burnett's, Coates, Tanqueray, Beefeater and Gilbey's. As consumers became aware of the quality and reputation of certain gin brands, distillers became increasingly keen to ensure the quality of their spirits once they left the distillery. Glass bottles, which are neutral compared to wooden casks, provided distillers with the vessel they were looking for. Due to the mechanical progress of the industrial revolution, the price of glass bottles, once prohibitively expensive, fell substantially. Then in 1860, Chancellor of the Exchequer, William Gladstone, passed the "Single Bottle Act" which allowed for the sale of gin by the bottle. This, in turn, allowed for alcohol consumption outside of licensed premises, paving the way for the modern liquor store.

Despite moving towards flavor-protective bottles, some companies actually introduced gins that had been matured in wood for a short time before bottling, emulating aspects of the gins of old. This was the first time that gin could be categorized as either white, i.e. no wood maturation, or yellow gin that had experienced a short maturation in wood, typically 3-4 weeks.

The most famous of these yellow gins was Booth's House of Lords Dry Gin or Booth's Finest Old Dry Gin, as it was known in the UK. Booth's was distilled at their distillery in Clerkenwell, London and was matured in wooden casks which were, at least at one point, ex-burgundy casks. Booth's discontinued their yellow gin in the mid 1970s. Noted drinks authors such as Anthony Haden-Guest, Kingsley Amis and David Embury, favored yellow gin. By the 1980s, yellow gin had disappeared, with one exception.

SEAGRAM'S GIN

The Seagram's family of Canada started making gin in 1857 by royal commission, although the gin we know today started its existence in the US in 1939. Bottled in the iconic bubbly bottle, Seagram's Ancient Gin was aged in white oak barrels that gave the gin its yellow color. Early advertisements extol the spirit's mellowed character and suggest mixing it with club soda as a permutation of the whiskey and soda.

Interestingly, Seagram's has never explicitly highlighted the fact that its gin is barrel-aged, only that it is "distinguished" and golden. However, in a brief period between the mid-1940s and early 1950s, bottles were adorned with small barrel charms—a nod to the secret of the gin's unusual character. In 1955, the name of the gin changed to "Seagram's Golden Gin," and in 1960, it was changed once again, to "Seagram's Extra Dry Golden Gin". Finally, in 1964, it was renamed for the last time, "Seagram's Extra Dry Gin."

In 2010, Seagram's stopped barrel-aging their Extra Dry Gin, citing a desire for greater quality control. However, the gin maintains it character and its color. On the label, the words "Barrel Mellowed for Smoothness since 1939" have been replaced with " Extra Smooth and Mellow since 1939." Some authors have speculated that a post-distillation infusion with juniper is part of the new production process. It is worth noting that the some of the Seagram's gin marketed for sale in Spain, prior to 2010, was both unaged and colorless.

CITADELLE GIN

Since the 1980s, things were quiet for yellow gin until 2008, when Alexandre Gabriel of Citadelle Gin released not only a new incarnation of yellow gin, aged in cognac barrels, but the first vintage yellow gin called Citadelle Reserve. His work was based on a French manuscript from 1775 written by Dunkirk-based gin distillers. For its 2008 vintage, Citadelle Reserve was an aged version of their classic gin (made using 19 botanicals). In subsequent years, the botanical mix was tinkered slightly to create a number of variations:

2009–Less impact of wood, made using a lower level of char on the barrel and a shorter maturation period.

2010–More floral, to complement the aging process; extra violet, iris and grains of paradise were used to make the gin, which was aged for 6 months in a barrel with a light char.

2011–The classic Citadelle botanicals were used.

2012–Three new botanicals: yuzu, genepi and cornflower, added to the original 19; the gin was then aged for 6 months in a barrel with a light char.

In 2013, things changed at Citadelle with the introduction of a solera system. The 2013 vintage was made of a blend of gins that had been aged in different barrels for a range of periods between 2 to 5 months. Some of the casks used include: American Oak—to add some vanilla, sweetness; ex-Pineau de Charente—for full-bodied floral notes; and ex-cognac. At any one time, only a portion of the gin will be removed from the barrels, which will then be topped up with Citadelle Gin. This replaces the vintage system and represents the end of Alexandre Gabriel's 5-year search to find his preferred method of making aged gin.

In 2011, Hayman's Distillers released their 1850 Reserve Gin. This was the first widely available yellow gin produced in the UK for over a century. The date in the name references a time before the single bottle act, which encouraged gin distillers to transition from barrels to glass bottles, and decreased the influence of wood on juniper.

BARREL TYPE

In the seventeenth century, barrels used to store gin would have been whatever was available and, as long as the barrel was in good order, the previous contents were not of any great concern. However, it is likely that most of the barrels would have previously contained sherry or port, as these were popular drinks at the time. Today, many craft distillers use ex-bourbon barrels. Because bourbon is legally required to be aged in a fresh barrel every time, there is a plentiful supply of used ones. In France and across continental Europe, ex-cognac casks are the preferred choice.

By 2013, distillers were paying greater attention to and experimented more with the range of flavors that previous fill barrels could impart on gin. Barrels that previously contained cocktails or cocktail bitters are a natural fit for aging a gin. California distilleries have taken advantage of the state's large wine industry by aging their gins in a variety of ex-wine casks. Distillery No. 209 has released two aged gins: one from sauvignon blanc casks and one from cabernet sauvignon casks. St. George released a variation of their Dry Rye Gin, which was aged in grenache and syrah barrels, and Old World Spirits' Rusty Blade Gin is aged in ex-wine casks made of French oak which imparts a different character than American oak.

Although oak is typically used in the production of whisky and many fortified wines, more exotic spirits such as cachaça are often aged in other woods, such as umburana, cedar and balsam. This offers another route for gin distillers to explore, such as one distiller who experimented with aging gin in barrels made from juniper wood. In addition to barrels and casks, it is not uncommon for producers to use oak alternatives such as wood chips or staves to add the wood notes they are looking for.

MATURATION

Maturation refers to the flavors that develop over time as a spirit is in contact with wood. Aging time and barrel size are the two most common variables that distillers manipulate to target their maturation profile. Aging time can range from a few weeks to over a decade in more extreme cases. Barrel size has a considerable impact upon maturation: the smaller the barrel, the more rapidly the wood will influence the flavor of the gin. This is due to the barrel having a greater surface area in contact with the spirit. For this reason, the use of staves or chips will increase the rate that wood character is imparted to a spirit. Like any spirit, char level, the previous use(s) of the barrel, and the conditions in which the barrel is kept (such a temperature and humidity level) will impact how the gin matures.

BOTANICAL MIX

As noted previously, there are two main approaches to the botanical mixes for yellow gin: the first uses the same botanical make-up as the distillery's standard dry gin, if one is produced; the second approach involves tailoring the botanical recipe specifically to enhance the harmony of the gin and the impact of the wood. Juniper tends to be emphasized and some distillers like to dial down the spice and citrus and increase the floral elements. It is also not unusual for an aged gin to be bottled at a higher ABV.

THE FLAVOR OF YELLOW GIN

....

ALAMBICS 13-YEAR OLD GIN (65.6% ABV)

Bottled at 65.6% ABV, this product is created in Scotland for a German company using a "well-established" gin as its base. It is distilled, matured and bottled in Scotland, but each run has just 272 bottles. It is aged for 11 years in old whisky barrels, before being finished for two years in ex-Caribbean Rum casks.

COLOR: Medium amber.

NOSE: Oak, vanilla, and treacle, with juniper at the very end.

TASTE: Smooth to start, with an almost sticky texture and notes of coriander and citrus, with a slight burnt orange biscuitiness. There's a growing strength, with a pine/juniper dryness appearing once you've swallowed, and continuing on a long finish.

....

BIG GIN BARREL AGED

Made by Captive Spirits of Seattle, the original BIG Gin is aged for

6 months in ex-whiskey barrels from Heaven Hill distillery.
COLOR: Pale straw.
NOSE: Sappy pine, beeswax with a hint of marmalade, then a swirl of spice.
TASTE: A lovely interplay between the gin and the wood. There are elements of wood sap, beeswax and resinous juniper. This is followed by some more intense spiciness such as a complex green cardamom, which moves on to a more mellow spice with vanilla and a light cinnamon, as well as some hints of wood. This is a sterling example of good balance in the interaction of spirit and barrel.

BOMBAY AMBER (47.0% ABV)

This aged gin is based on the same mix of eight botanicals that are used to make Bombay Dry Gin, plus the addition of nutmeg, toasted black cardamom, and bitter orange zest. Like other Bombay gins, it is distilled via vapour infusion using a botanical basket. The resultant gin is then rested in French ex-vermouth barrels.
COLOR: Straw gold.
NOSE: Reminds me of a Martini: there are the dry, juniper elements from the gin, but there's also a slightly sweet spiciness and a herbal note, as well as a hint of oxidized citrus, reminiscent of a white vermouth.
TASTE: Smooth, but with a strong flavor: lots of rich, spiced notes, along with a touch of pepper/menthol. Jammy, zesty orange is followed by a plumper, herbal impression: juniper, coriander, and then some woody notes. Lots of the vermouth's character comes through in the spirit, giving it a great complexity that is present all the way through to the finish.

BREUCKELEN DISTILLERY - GLORIOUS GIN (45.0% ABV)

The two gins described below were each aged for 90 days in identical barrels of equal size and char. Both barrels were kept in an area of the New York distillery without climatic controls. The difference between the two was that one was aged during the winter, whilst the other was aged during the summer, each experiencing the opposite extreme temperatures of New York's seasons.

Winter Aged
COLOR: Straw yellow.
NOSE: Fairly spicy, with hints of fruit salad and grapefruit.
TASTE: Quite citrusy with notes of fizzy lemon, herbs, wood and sweet vanilla towards the end. The finish tastes of ginger and a little spicy cinnamon. This gin seems more dominant over the effects of the wood, making this well suited to mixing in long summer drinks.

Summer Aged
COLOR: Dark amber-gold.
NOSE: More spicy than the winter aged variety, but with

more citrus, as well.

TASTE: Notes of dark chocolate and powerful oak, followed by a dry, spicy finish. There are some deeper, herbal notes and mellow citrus, too. The wood notes here are more dominant than those of the gin, but add a greater complexity to the spirit. Excellent for Old Fashioneds and short drinks.

BURROUGH'S RESERVE (43.0% ABV)

This gin is made using the classic Beefeater recipe with one of the original stills of James Burrough. The spirit is then aged for a few months in Jean de Lillet casks.

COLOR: A very light straw gold.

NOSE: Juniper, orange, dark caramel and woody spice.

TASTE: A soft texture, with plenty of vanilla, cinnamon, and nutmeg upfront. Whilst quite sweet to start, this moves on to dryer, slightly tannin-like flavors, then the classic juniper and angelica gin flavors with a little citrus, before finishing with some vanilla, oak notes.

CITADELLE RESERVE (44.0% ABV)

2008 *Vintage*

COLOR: Straw yellow, like Lillet Blanc.

NOSE: Thick, floral anise and juniper, with some sweetness.

TASTE: Oak and vanilla came through, resulting in a taste almost halfway between whisky and gin.

2010 *Vintage*

COLOR: Straw yellow, like Lillet Blanc.

NOSE: Perfumed, with notes of juniper and lemongrass.

TASTE: Juniper, followed by floral notes: lavender, violet and some rose. This is much more perfumed, with higher notes than in the 2008 vintage with a very discernible difference.

2013 *Solera*

COLOR: Very pale, golden straw.

NOSE: Dry juniper, citrus and a hint of brine.

TASTE: Floral upfront, with more intense notes of freshly cracked black pepper. Very vibrant, bright and exciting: violet petals in the middle of the profile, along with other spiced notes and orange towards the end. Also, dry cinnamon and a touch of turmeric. Superb.

COLOMBIAN ORTODOXY AGED GIN (43.0% ABV)

This gin is distilled five times at Distileria Colombiana in Cartagena, on the northern coast of Columbia. The distillery opened in 1913 and also makes Dictador Rum. The gin is aged in their used rum casks for at least 6 months. Before bottling, the aged gin is filtered to remove the color, but keep the flavor, similar to the technique used to make aged white rums.

COLOR: Clear.

NOSE: Juniper, orange and a hint of creamy vanilla and molasses.

TASTE: A good texture, with juniper upfront and then fresh citrus oil, with orange in particular. This makes way for a little licorice and then some more herbaceous and spiced notes, followed by a floral flourish of orange blossom and lemongrass, culminating in a long, lingering, dry finish of citrus and juniper.

COLOMBIAN TREASURE AGED GIN (43.0 %ABV)

Using the Limon Mandarino as a primary botanical, the base for this spirit is made from sugar cane. The gin is then aged for 35 weeks in ex-rum casks.

COLOR: Amber.

NOSE: Very citrusy: tangerine, orange, lemon, and a little sweetness. There are then some leafy, herbal notes and a hint of woody vanilla.

TASTE: This is a thick and viscous spirit: warm and full of citrus notes; rich, complex marmalade; and warm, woody notes that remind me of high-end triple sec brands, such as Grand Marnier or Combier. Finally, there's a lovely warm and cozy finish of warm, woody spice.

DISTILLERY NO. 209 CABERNET SAUVIGNON BARREL-AGED GIN (46.0% ABV)

The original No. 209 gin aged for over 3 months in oak that once held Rudd Cabernet Sauvignon.

COLOR: Golden brown, almond shell.

NOSE: Cardamom, notes of Madeira and Sherry; hints of lemon and citrus. Smooth, subtle gin hint on nose. Very interesting; milder than most aged gins.

TASTE: Oily citrus and cinnamon at first; builds quickly. Full bodied in the middle. Robust juniper, pepper, heat, baking spices. Finishes with oaky tinge and sherry, oxidized fruit, grapes, apple. Smooth the whole way through.

DISTILLERY NO. 209 SAUVIGNON BLANC BARREL-AGED GIN (46.0% ABV)

The original No. 209 gin aged for over 3 months in French oak that once held Rudd Sauvignon Blanc.

COLOR: Pale straw, and almost exactly the color of a Chardonnay.

NOSE: Disarmingly quiet. Stone fruit and juniper, lemon peel and a bit of alcohol.

TASTE: Again, quiet at first. Lemon and orange peel, bright stone fruit with coriander and juniper in the mid-notes. Creamy and buttery finish, citrus tinge, cardamom and oak. Touch of acidity on the finish.

FEW BARREL-AGED GIN (46.5% ABV)

FEW Barrel-Aged Gin is made using a specific botanical recipe, with the aim of complementing the notes and flavors that the wood will impart on the spirit. There is a greater focus on floral notes to match the sweetness that the wood adds, as well as extra juniper to maintain the gin's character.

COLOR: Light amber orange.

NOSE: Sweet wood and mint, reminiscent of bourbon.

TASTE: Dark sugar and treacle, minty wood, and licorice. Good doses of sweet spice, gingerbread and ginger cake, as well as notes of candied peel. All-round, this is a charming product, still reminiscent of the original's gin character, but with the impact of the wood definitely coming through.

FEW BARREL-AGED CASK STRENGTH GIN (58.5%ABV)

COLOR: Bright, golden yellow.

NOSE: Lemon, grain, coriander, grapefruit, juniper and a touch of spice.

TASTE: Surprisingly smooth for the strength, with strong notes of lemon and grapefruit, mixed with piney juniper. Towards the end, the effects of the wood come through as dry spice and black tea with just a touch of coconut. Powerful and complex, with a finish that highlights the balance of gin and wood.

FILLIERS BARREL-AGED GIN (43.7 % ABV)

This is an aged version of the Belgium Distiller's Dry 28 Gin, which is aged around 6 months in ex-cognac casks.

COLOR: Pale yellow.

NOSE: Soft, cut flowers, bitter orange and some spicy fruitiness.

TASTE: An interplay of classic gin flavors: juniper, coriander, anise, licorice, and citrus–all intermingled with a subtle sweetness, spice, and wood notes, such as vanilla, cassia and a touch of grape.

GINNIFER GOLDEN GIN (49.0% ABV)

Made by Great Southern Distillery of Albany, Western Australia, this starts with their grape-based Great Southern Dry Gin, which is made using a blend of nine botanicals: juniper, coriander, angelica, lemon, orris root, cardamom, cinnamon, anise and meen (bloodroot). It is then aged in French oak barriques.

COLOR: Golden yellow.

NOSE: Citrus, angelica, and coriander, with a little dry spice. Vanilla, pepper, and a touch of black tea.

TASTE: Viscous and oily, the initial, classic flavors of this gin–juniper, angelica, and citrus that move onto the sweeter, woody flavors of vanilla, nutmeg, and cinnamon. However, the flavors then move back to a long, dry finish of juniper and citrus.

GREENHAT GINAVIT (FALL/WINTER SEASONAL GIN) (45.2% ABV)

This seasonal gin from Columbia Distillers in Washington D.C. is a mix of typical gin botanicals (juniper, coriander, celery seed, fennel seed, angelica, orris root, cinnamon, grains of paradise, lemon and orange) and typical aquavit botanicals (caraway seed, fresh dill, star anise), using a wheat and rye base which is then aged in ex-applejack barrels for around 3 months.

COLOR: Very pale straw gold.

NOSE: Hints of maple, fennel, caraway, rye bread, and some floral elements. Celery and black pepper, too.

TASTE: Juniper upfront, plus a little angelica; sweet black licorice in the middle, some notes of vanilla and maple, and an element of fennel and caraway bread. This is intensely flavored with an unusual botanical mix, but it works in harmony with the wood, making it an excellent example of an aged gin.

HAMMER & SONS OLD ENGLISH AGED GIN

A unique approach to yellow gin: rather than aging in-house, Henrik Hammer decided to give the casks directly to bartenders. These 5-liter casks made from French oak, medium toast, are emblazoned with the Hammer & Sons crest and allow bartenders to experiment with aging gin themselves.

3 weeks

COLOR: Clear, with a hint of pale straw.

NOSE: Spicy, with plenty of cardamom and cinnamon, followed by slightly savory elements; before, some classic dry botanicals such as juniper, coriander and angelica, as well as a touch of floral flair.

TASTE: Dry spiciness upfront: cassia, with a little capsicum and black pepper, followed by some rich, fresh and resinous juniper. There is a little sweetness in the middle, but it is very subtle. The barrel's notes really come through towards the end, mixed with a little dry juniper, plenty of clean, woody elements, nutmeg, cinnamon, and vanilla.

7 weeks

COLOR: Very pale straw.

NOSE: Rich citrus: lemon, orange, and coriander, followed by dry, woody spice and a little vanilla pod. Overall, dry with a little wood.

TASTE: A rich and full texture with a little, sugary sweetness upfront, mixed with cinnamon and nutmeg and then a sweetness that reminds me of licorice root. This is followed by some dryness and a hint of leafiness, before a warm, well-rounded and spicy finish, reminiscent of the best sipping spirits.

HAYMAN'S 1850 RESERVE GIN (40.0% ABV)

Launched in June 2011, this yellow gin is rested in ex-whisky casks for around 3 to 4 weeks. It uses a different botanical mix from that of the classic Hayman's London Dry Gin, resulting in increased

notes of herbs and spices.
COLOR: A clear and very pale, straw yellow.
NOSE: Juniper, with some spice and hints of floral notes.
TASTE: Juniper, floral, and a light bite of citrus, before a smooth, mellow finish with a hint of creamy vanilla. Smooth and subtle.

HDC DISTILLERS RESERVE AGED SOFT GIN (62.5% ABV)
Produced at the Heritage Distilling Company in Washington, USA. This uses HDC's grape-based, botanically-infused Soft Gin at cask strength as a base, which is then aged in oak barrels.
COLOR: Warm, golden raisin.
NOSE: Vanilla, treacle, rich fruit cake, and spice.
TASTE: Dark fruitcake, followed by a blend of root and birch beer, then a dry finish. There are some complex, woody notes beyond the usual oak and vanilla. Overall, this is a unique spirit that is surprisingly smooth, given its high ABV.

HEALY'S RESERVE (43.0% ABV)
Trailhead Spirit from Billings, Montana produces Healy's Reserve. It is based on the original Healy's Gin, which is then aged in used oak whiskey barrels.
COLOR: Warm straw.
NOSE: Spice and a little sour crispness, like a fresh, good quality scrumpy cider.
TASTE: This has a smooth texture, with dry juniper upfront and then some fruity citrus, coriander, and some spiced notes from the botanicals and wood. This is followed by notes of rose, with a little hops and breadiness on the finish.

HERNÖ JUNIPER CASK (47.0% ABV)
This is made using Hernö Swedish Excellence Gin which is aged in a barrel made of juniper wood (Juniperus Occidentalis) from the USA. The barrels are Ankares, which is an old, Swedish barrel unit, equivalent to 39.25 liters. Because of the limited volume of the barrels, the first batch was limited to 87 bottles.
COLOR: Light lemon/straw yellow.
NOSE: Lemon and orange, followed by a progression of crisp pine notes, woody notes of juniper and a little sappiness. Intense, inviting and engaging.
TASTE: A rich, smooth and silky–almost honey-like–texture. There's an herbal sweetness to start, before moving onto a light, green juniper note, followed by a darker, heavy flavor of juniper and rich, bold pine notes. Finally, there's some citrus peel and a little woody sappiness. On the finish there is resinous pine, a hint of beeswax, citrus peel and a touch of coriander.

JODHPUR RESERVE (43.0% ABV)

UK's Langley Distillers makes a high-strength version of the classic Jodhpur London Dry Gin for the Spanish Market. The gin is made using 11 botanicals: juniper, coriander, angelica, lemon, orange, orris root, almond, cassia, licorice, ginger and grapefruit. It is then aged in ex-Spanish brandy casks made out of American white oak.

COLOR: Golden yellow.

NOSE: Lots of juniper, some woody notes, and a floral spice.

TASTE: An absolutely superb texture: smooth, with a touch of viscosity; creamy vanilla makes way for some pine and coriander, followed by hints of maple, vanilla and wood. This has a very good balance and there is a great interplay between the wood and gin.

MYRTLE GIN (47.0%ABV)

Produced in Glasgow for the Spirit of the Coquet, Myrtle Gin is a Scottish gin that has been aged for 10 years and infused with Northumberland Myrtle.

COLOR: Deep amber-brown, rather like apple juice.

NOSE: Initially, wood and Scotch whisky, then some smokiness, akin to the smoke of smoked salmon, then some vanilla notes and a floral-herbal mix.

TASTE: Full of flavor at the start: woody, followed by leafy, herbal notes and a growing, peaty character towards the end. The finish is of dry juniper and long lasting.

NEW YORK DISTILLING AGED PERRY'S TOT NAVY STRENGTH GIN (57.0% ABV)

This is an aged version of New York Distilling's Navy Strength Gin. It is available exclusively at the distillery's on-site bar, The Shanty.

COLOR: Pale ochre.

NOSE: Oak and coriander.

TASTE: Well-rounded, with plenty of oak and spice, such as cinnamon. There is also some coriander notes and sweetness. Comparing this with the unaged spirit provides a great example of how effective barrel aging can be to a gin.

OLD GROVE BARREL-RESTED (44.0% ABV)

This is made by Ballast Point Distillery in San Diego, CA and is based on their original Old Grove Gin, which has then been aged for around 50 days in American oak.

COLOR: Warm gold.

NOSE: Soft cinnamon, oak, vanilla, and a little dryness.

TASTE: A good balance between the flavors of the gin and those of the wood. Additional spiced elements appear, notably: cedar, cinnamon, nutmeg, and a little pepper. This is a well-integrated example of an aged gin.

ORIGINAL FINISHED IN CHERRY BRANDY CASK (43.0% ABV)

A dry gin from Scheibel Distillery in Kappelrodeck, Germany, which is aged in a cask that has previously stored cherry brandy. This process was discovered by accident when distiller Michael Scheibel took a hip flask of cherry brandy on a trip to the UK. When the brandy had all gone, he filled the flask with gin and liked the resulting combination of flavors.

COLOR: Rose gold.

NOSE: Juniper and angelica upfront, followed by spice, including cinnamon and vanilla. This develops into mellow, woody notes and a hint of cherry stone. Complex and inviting.

TASTE: Very flavorsome with an initial burst of vanilla and pine, followed by sweeter spice and fruity, confectionary notes; the cherry really comes through and the flavors remind me of a home-baked cherry cobbler. The profile then moves back to the gin, with more juniper, angelica, citrus, and floral notes, including violet. A warm finish with dried cherry stone and light, warming oak, as well as a woody dryness.

PROFESSOR CORNELIUS AMPLEFORTH'S ANGLO-SCOTTISH-AMERICAN GIN (67.5%ABV)

Part of an experimental range released by the professor, this gin takes Scottish malt spirit and re-distills it with botanicals under a vacuum. The spirit is then aged in England in a cask previously used for a batch of FEW Barrel-Aged American Gin.

COLOR: Yellow-white.

NOSE: Quite creamy, with vanilla notes followed by a hint of dry spice, reminiscent of homemade custard or crème anglais.

TASTE: Powerful spirit, but also rather smooth and an almost liqueur-like texture to begin with, along with a creaminess, courtesy of the barley spirit base. There is a fair amount of sweetness, and the spice of a dry gingerbread cookie. The finish is more gin-like, with citrus and juniper. A very long, winding finish.

PROFESSOR CORNELIUS AMPLEFORTH'S CASK AGED GIN (43.3%ABV)

This is an aged version of the Professor's Bathtub Gin, a cold-compounded gin, i.e. infused with botanicals and not distilled with them. It is then aged until it is ready, typically between 3-6 months, in Octave casks, which are around a fifth of the size of a hogshead cask (300 liters).

COLOR: Light amber.

NOSE: Dry wood and vanilla. This is incredibly dry, with just a hint of mature cheddar cheese and coconut.

TASTE: Like the nose, this is dry, with wood upfront, followed by juniper, angelica and citrus. There are then more spicy notes of cassia, nutmeg and vanilla. All of the spice notes are dry, not sweet.

[*Yellow Gin*]

PROFESSOR CORNELIUS AMPLEFORTH'S BATHTUB NAVY CASK GIN (57.0% ABV)

An aged version of the Professor's Navy Gin, it aged for around 6 months in American oak casks.

COLOR: Dark, rich gold.

NOSE: Dry Christmas spice: cinnamon, cassia, nutmeg and cloves, but a little woody vanilla, too. Softer than the nose for the regular Bathtub Navy Gin.

TASTE: Superb–has a texture that just expands in your mouth, something that's really rather different. It's also rather smooth for 57% ABV. There's lots of spice upfront, with a slightly confectionary quality, reminiscent of Easter cake or a Tiffin Slice (or light Christmas pudding). Finally, there's an unusual finish of sarsaparilla, cherry and almond, with just a hint of pine sap.

PROFESSOR CORNELIUS AMPLEFORTH'S BITTERS-AGED BATHTUB GIN (43.3% ABV)

The professor took a batch of Bathtub Gin and aged it for three months in a 20-liter cask that had previously held cask-aged bitters.

COLOR: Warm gold.

NOSE: Lots of spice, nutmeg, cinnamon and cassia.

TASTE: Sweetness upfront, then plenty of confectionary cinnamon and cassia, reminiscent of Christmas spiced cookies and pumpkin pie. Finally, there is some more intense bitterness and the juniper comes through. Extremely intense in flavor, this has plenty of mixing potential.

PROFESSOR CORNELIUS AMPLEFORTH'S NEGRONI-AGED BATHTUB GIN (43.3% ABV)

The professor has also aged some Bathtub Gin for three months in a 50-liter cask that had previously held a batch of Negroni cocktail.

COLOR: Rose gold.

NOSE: Juniper and some strong, herbal woody notes.

TASTE: This is a spicy gin with both a little sweetness and the bold bitterness that you would expect from a Negroni. It has a very mellow flavor overall, but the character of the Negroni from the barrel really comes through. Sipping-wise, it is very balanced and intriguing.

PROFESSOR CORNELIUS AMPLEFORTH'S OLD FASHIONED-AGED BATHTUB GIN (43.3% ABV)

The latest addition to the Professor's range of creatively-aged gins, this has been matured in a 50 liter cask that had previously contained a batch of Old Fashioned cocktail.

COLOR: Medium-honey.

NOSE: Honey and orange, with hints of spice and whiskey, much like a good whiskey liqueur.

TASTE: Very soft, velvety, and full-bodied. There are wood notes upfront, with sweetness and spice, as well as a touch of whisky smoke and burnt orange. The flavor then shifts to more traditional gin notes: juniper, angelica, citrus, and a slightly floral flair, somewhat reminiscent of violets and root beer.

ROUNDHOUSE IMPERIAL (47.0% ABV)

Made by Roundhouse Spirits in Boulder, Colorado, the Imperial Gin is an aged version of the classic Roundhouse Gin. It is aged for at least 6 months in new oak barrels but, as with all aged gins, the main time frame is "when it's ready."

COLOR: Light pumpkin.

NOSE: Sweet and spicy, with hints of freshly cracked black pepper and a little green anise.

TASTE: Sweet cordial anise, a bit like Pernod pastis. It is slightly reminiscent of the historical Sir Walt's Liqueur: a broad collection of herbal flavors, with peppermint, licorice and a faint whiff of wood sap. Anise and the lively, fresh black pepper are on the finish. Delicious.

RUSTY BLADE (62.0% ABV)

Released in 2010, Rusty Blade, produced by Old World Spirits, is made from a batch of their classic Blade Gin that has been aged in French oak casks.

COLOR: Burnt orange.

NOSE: Botanically intense, this is very spicy with cinnamon, orange and lemon.

TASTE: Nutmeg, cinnamon, and orange, with a hint of raisin, making this somewhat reminiscent of a cinnamon and raisin Danish pastry. The finish consists of concentrated flavors, like aromatic bitters.

SEAGRAM'S DISTILLER'S RESERVE (51.0% ABV)

Introduced in 2006 and bottled at 51.0% ABV, Distiller's Reserve is more intense as a result of its higher alcoholic strength, which helps the botanical aromatics shine through. The reduction in dilution also means that the effect of the barrel is more pronounced.

COLOR: Very light straw yellow.

NOSE: The nose seems less intense than the original, with some juniper and citrus.

TASTE: Firstly, the texture is quite different: viscous, silky and smooth–unusually smooth for a gin at 51% ABV. As well as juniper, there are sweet licorice notes, in addition to floral and citrus flavors.

SEAGRAM'S EXTRA DRY GIN (40.0% ABV)

This pre-2010 bottling of the gin was distilled at a low temperature with botanicals, including juniper, coriander, angelica, orange, cardamom and cassia. The gin was then matured in white-oak casks.

COLOR: Very light straw yellow.

NOSE: Quite light; juniper with coriander and citrus.

TASTE: Smooth, with notes of juniper, coriander and a touch of orange. Similar to a normal London Dry Gin, with a slight mellow note of creamy, vanilla/oak, but it seems like the wood has more of an effect on the texture than the flavor.

SMOOTH AMBLER STILLHOUSE COLLECTION BARREL GIN (49.5% ABV)

Made by the Smooth Ambler Distillery in Greenbrier County, West Virginia, this uses the Greenbrier Gin as a base, which is aged for three months in a combination of virgin barrels and ex-bourbon barrels from the distillery's own Old Scout Bourbon.

COLOR: Golden amber.

NOSE: Hops, vanilla and dry juniper.

TASTE: Spicy to start. Hints of anise, dewy pine and juniper are followed by an earthy woodiness and gradually building bitterness on the finish.

SPY HOP (42.0% ABV)

This is based on Spy Hop Gin, which is made using botanicals that include juniper, lemon, star anise, cardamom, orris root, blackberries, wild roses, and lavender. The gin is aged in an 8-gallon oak barrel for two months, and then bottled with a curl of madrone bark.

COLOR: Mid-straw.

NOSE: Perfumed, with notes of juniper, coriander, warm spice and cedar.

TASTE: Starts out quite perfumed, with coriander and some of the floral notes that you would associate with fruit eau de vies; this then makes way for woody, spiced notes from the aging process.

ST. GEORGE DRY RYE RESPOSADO GIN (49.5% ABV)

Made by the St. George Distillery in Alameda, California, this gin uses their rye-based gin, "Dry Rye," as a base. This is then aged in casks previously used for syrah and grenache.

COLOR: Rich copper.

NOSE: A strong nose packed full of intrigue: lots of dry, woody pine with resin, but also some stone fruit and a more woody fruitiness. As the spirit opens up, subtle nutty notes, lime citrus, and pepper come through.

TASTE: Even more complex and indulgent on the taste than on the nose. The rich fruitiness of the wine cask mingles with a little soft spice; this is followed by resinous and bright juniper, pine and, finally, a warmer fruitiness. This is a multi-facetted gin and well worth exploring.

STRATHEARN OAKED HIGHLAND GIN (40.0% ABV)

Made by the Strathearn Distillery in Perthshire, Scotland, this is a distilled gin that has been infused with vanilla and shavings from oak Scotch whisky casks for 10 days.

COLOR: Mid-straw.

NOSE: Light wood and vanilla, white chocolate and juicy citrus. Very aromatic.

TASTE: Quite sweet, especially upfront, with plenty of vanilla, cinnamon, and both milk and white chocolate, combined with sweet rose. This moves onto some dryer flavours of citrus, coriander, angelica, and a floral element. A bold and warming spirit with a strong, confectionary character.

COCKTAILS

Yellow gin was originally used in exactly the same way as regular (white) gin and, as such, there is no one drink that stands out as being the quint-essential yellow gin cocktail. However, the use of yellow gin does make a notable difference in the following classic gin drinks.

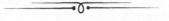

Gin & Tonic

In comparison to using white gin, the yellow gin adds a richer and more complex flavor profile with hints of wood, spice and vanilla. At the same time, the crispness of the dry juniper and other botanicals comes through, along with all of the refreshment you'd expect from the drink. This is truly the Rolls Royce of Gin & Tonics.

2 parts yellow gin
5 parts Fevertree tonic water
Add ingredients to a chilled tumbler with plenty of ice.

Martini

With white gin, the drink is crisp and refreshing with a clean dryness, but the use of yellow gin allows a warm, spiced complexity to come through, almost reminiscent of fine whisky or brandy. At the same time, the herbal elements of the vermouth bring out the citrus of the gin, adding a crisp freshness that makes the drink the perfect pre-dinner cocktail.

50 ml yellow gin
10 ml dry vermouth
Stir

.

4

Hollands Gin

During the nineteenth century, cocktail recipes usually called for one of three gin styles: London dry, epitomized by brands such as Beefeater, Tanqueray and Gordon's; Old Tom, the sweetened style of gin, as described in chapter one; and Hollands gin.

Hollands gin is similar to Geneva or jeneva, the ancestor of dry gin, which comes from the area of Europe in and around the Netherlands, Belgium and Germany. Unlike dry gin, which is made from neutral grain spirits, traditional or oude genever tends to be partially made with malt wine. And korenwijn, an even older style of gin, contains even more malt wine in its base, which gives korenwijn a malty, whisky-like character.

Similarly, Hollands gin typically contains a good proportion of malt wine in its spirit base and has a narrower range of botanicals used to flavor it. It was common to find examples of Hollands gin that were only flavored with juniper, or juniper plus one or two other subtle signature flavors.

At one time, this style of gin was made all over the world. The availability of grain in the US made it a popular style. New York, the former Dutch colony known as New Amsterdam, produced a large supply of Hollands gin. As public tastes moved toward the cleaner, dryer flavors of dry gin following the Second World War, Hollands, like Old Tom, became increasingly obscure until it was only available in the form of Geneva from its home countries. Even then, it was rarely exported.

THE FLAVOR OF HOLLANDS GIN

NEW YORK DISTILLING CHIEF GOWANUS NEW-NETHERLAND GIN (44.0%)

In 2013, New York Distilling, based in Brooklyn, New York, released a Hollands gin in collaboration with drink historian David Wondrich. Chief Gowanus New-Netherland Gin uses a double-distilled, un-aged rye whiskey as its base and is flavored with juniper and a handful of cluster hops. The spirit is also aged in oak barrels for three months.

COLOR: Oaked white wine.

NOSE: Full, bready grain, with fennel and dark chocolate.

TASTE: A little sweetness upfront, then the initial character of the grain and then the juniper, dry pine and citrus. Rich, sweet and spicy notes appear with cocoa, fennel, and dry cassia, followed by a long, dry finish of bitter anise. This has a full and warming texture, but without burn, making it comforting and cozy.

COCKTAILS

Noted authors David Embury, John Doxat and a few more, state that Hollands gin does not tend to mix well and is therefore best consumed on its own. Nonetheless, it was used in a number of examples.

———— ○ ————

John Collins

The John Collins is the archetypal cocktail of Hollands gin and many aficionados would argue that, if you replace it with any other type of gin, then your cocktail is not a true John Collins. When compared to a Collins made with dry gin, the Hollands version is noticeably sweeter, with more substantial body, maltiness and strong juniper. It is a hearty drink with a warming, yet refreshing quality.

2 parts Hollands gin
1 part fresh lemon juice
1 part sugar syrup
6 parts club soda
Stir

Silver Cocktail

This is a dry drink with good qualities as an aperitif and, although it is a drink of substance, it is lighter than many other Hollands gin drinks.

Equal parts Hollands gin and French vermouth
2 dashes orange bitters
2 dashes Maraschino
Stir

Yachting Club

Peychaud's and absinthe work well with the strong herbal notes of Hollands gin, making a very nice cocktail. Alternatively, when dry gin is substituted, this drink can fall flat, lacking the substance and body of the original.

2 parts Holland gin
1 part French vermouth
2 dashes Peychaud's bitters
1 dash absinthe
Stir

Night Cap

(Old Fashioned, substituting Hollands gin for whiskey).
Making this using a dry gin produces a good drink with plenty of flavor, some sweetness, spice and a dry finish. However, when using Hollands gin, the drink becomes far more complex, with rich flavors of malt and herbs in addition to the spice. Very intense, this is a notable rival to a whiskey Old Fashioned.

4 parts Holland gin
2 dashes Angostora bitters
2 dashes sugar syrup
Stir

5

Flavored Gin

One of the broadest and least appreciated areas of long-lost spirits and liqueurs is that of flavored or cordial gin. Over the past century, distillers all over the world have produced more than a dozen different cordial gins. These gins were typically made by steeping ingredients in spirit before sweetening, resulting in a liquor that was part-spirit and part-liqueur, hence the term "cordial." Historically, cordial spirits were bottled at around 25-30% ABV. The two most popular flavors used in the production of cordial gins were orange and lemon. There was also a product, known as "Rue" gin, that combined both of these citrus flavors.

ORANGE GIN

Orange gin was the most popular flavored gin of its time; orange-flavored brandy, genever and whisky were also once common and widely available. Orange gin dates from the early twentieth century and is mentioned in Hugo R. Ensslin's 1917 cocktail book. The most successful brand of orange gin, during its popularity, was Gordon's, which was manufactured between 1929 and 1988.

Traditionally, distillers made orange gin by infusing orange fruit, typically the peel, in gin and then adding sugar. Some more modern versions are colorless and the orange flavor is added via essences and flavorings rather than infusion. Examples include an orange flavored gin made by Beefeater (1980s-1990s) bottled at 40% ABV, and another produced by Seagram's, which is still in production.

At the time of writing, no company makes a commercial orange gin that is faithful to the style of the early twentieth century, although Chase of England makes an excellent Seville Orange Marmalade Gin and Spencerfield Spirits of Scotland makes a Spiced Orange Gin Liqueur. Despite this current lack of commercial orange gins, its production is not complicated. The recipe supplied in Appendix II can be easily made at home.

THE FLAVOR OF ORANGE GIN

DAVID'S ORANGE GIN
COLOR: Light orange.
NOSE: Rich and aromatic, zesty orange.
TASTE: Dry and intense, with the aromas of the orange oil coming through, as well as some floral notes, reminiscent of orange blossom. It is both mixable and sippable.

LEMON GIN

Lemon gin was second only to orange gin in its popularity, a fact that might be reversed today, given the modern palate's appetite for tartness. At one time the great gin houses—Gordon's, Tanqueray, Booth's and Plymouth—amongst others made lemon gin.

It is interesting that there is no evidence of lime gin dating back to the late-nineteenth and early-twentieth centuries; however, that flavor is much more popular today. A variety of lime gins are available today from Seagram's, Tanqueray, Ish Gin from England, and Gin Lubuski from Poland. This is likely due to a relatively recent transformation in public tastes towards a preference for the more sour flavor of lime over the sweeter lemon.

Gordon's introduced their lemon gin in 1931 and produced it until 1988. Beefeater also made a lemon-flavored gin in the 1980s, but no known lemon gin remains in production today. However, a historically inspired recipe for lemon gin can be found in Appendix II and revived from oblivion.

THE FLAVOR OF LEMON GIN

....

DAVID'S LEMON GIN
COLOR: Light lemon yellow.
NOSE: Fresh, crisp, zesty lemon.
TASTE: A very flavorful gin with notes of tart lemon and a hint of cardamom spice. The finish is dry, with juniper and other botanicals from the base gin coming through over time.

APPLE GIN

T.E. Carling described Apple gin in *The Complete Book of Drink*, published in 1951, as being popular in the United Kingdom, especially in Scotland. Today, this flavored gin has become rather obscure but, given the almost universal appeal of the flavor of apple, it seemed worthy of inclusion in this book. *The Café Royal Cocktail Book* of 1937 states that apple gin was available in two varieties: sweet and dry. Like its flavored gin contemporaries, apple gin was simply gin infused with apple. The sweet variety had a little added sugar, whilst the dry version remained unsweetened.

While apple has not been completely estranged from gin, there are no commercial gins using apple like the historic examples described above. Seagram's currently make an "apple-twisted" gin; though, in contrast to the historical recipes, this is flavored with essence. An example that better reflects the historical style is the Apple Jenever made by Filliers of Belgium. It is worth noting that apple is currently used as a botanical in Caoruun Gin from Scotland and Elephant Gin from Germany. William Chase, Bellewood and CapRock also use it to produce their base spirit for their gins.

Some recipes for traditional Scottish-style apple gin can be found in Appendix II. It should be pointed out that the variety of apple used to make apple gin has a great impact on the flavor.

THE FLAVOR OF APPLE GIN

....

DAVID'S BRAMLEY APPLE GIN
NOSE: Marzipan, almond and slightly sour apple.

TASTE: Quite pleasant, with a lot of character; an initial honey sweetness, vanilla and then sharp, crisp, sour apple on the finish.

DAVID'S KATY APPLE GIN

NOSE: Although this was the lightest in color of the apple gins tested here, it had a very intense nose, being slightly salty with some nutty elements, too.

TASTE: Certainly dryer, this was slightly vermouth-like, with a quite tart, but creamy finish. The taste is quite odd, with a very different style.

DAVID'S WORCHESTER APPLE GIN

NOSE: A rich amber in color, this had an even stronger nose, more like cider. It was also dryer, with some citrus and almond, in addition to the apple.

TASTE: Very smooth, with an almost honey-like texture. Fresh apple notes, followed by warmer cream and vanilla notes, reminiscent of spiced baked apple. The juniper of the gin comes through at the end.

MINT GIN

The quest for long, lost cocktail ingredients sometimes provides an interesting snapshot of the changing tastes of the drinking public. One of the best examples of this is mint gin. This once popular cordial gin brings to mind a vibrant green liqueur with the minty fresh flavor of mouthwash, like many of the mass-produced Crème de Menthes have today. However, if a mint gin had a balanced flavor, the herbal and crisp elements of the mint leaves could add a refreshing quality to many mixed drinks.

In the early part of the twentieth century, many of the American "spirits houses," such as Old Mr. Boston, Piping Rock and Jacquins, all had a mint-flavored gin in their product portfolio. During Prohibition, the strong mint flavor and added sugar was a good way of concealing poor quality spirit.

Originally, mint gin was a simple infusion of gin with mint leaves, which added both flavor and color to the spirit. However, producers of mint gin eventually switched to using flavor essences and artificial colorings instead. This is evident by the fact that some examples of mint gin still retain their lurid shade of green, despite being over half a century old.

Gordon's and Baffert's made the most recent examples of mint gin. Gordon's released their Spearmint gin in the 1980s; at this time they were also producing a grapefruit-flavored gin. Also, Baffert's made a mint gin in the 1990s. Both were colorless and flavored with essences.

THE FLAVOR OF MINT GIN

DAVID'S PEPPERMINT GIN

NOSE: Menthol, with hints of vanilla and a little lemon.

TASTE: Leafy peppermint, with some sweetness. This had a bold flavor that would stand up well to mixing in cocktails, but was less accessible when drinking neat.

Recipes of how to make mint gin can be found in Appendix II.

OTHER FLAVORS

In his 1951 cocktail book, T.E. Carling mentions the existence of blackberry gin and damson gin, both of which are still available, as well as bullace gin and ginger gin. These were all cordial gins made by infusion, with added sugar. In the US, evidence exists for a wide variety of other, unusual flavors, although a lot less is written about them in cocktail books. And recently Brennan & Brown, a distillery in Cheltenham, UK, released a modern version of a botanically intense ginger gin.

ASPARAGUS GIN

Produced by the Folsom Asparagus Gin Company of San Francisco and bottled at 30% ABV, this was made by compounding asparagus with gin that was distilled elsewhere. Sadly, the Asparagus Gin Company only operated between 1916 and 1918.

PINEAPPLE GIN

A pineapple gin called "Dinner at Eight," was produced in the 1950s by the Distillers Distributing Corporation of San Francisco. It was slightly stronger than other flavored gins of the day, being bottled at 40% ABV. It is notable that the label says the company "prepares and bottles" the gin, suggesting that the gin was brought in and the pineapple and sugar added afterwards.

MAPLE GIN

Buffalo Distilling in Buffalo, NY, manufactured a maple gin from the late nineteenth century to the early twentieth century, at a time when liquor was often sold as a remedy to various ailments. For maple gin, which was specifically aimed at women, the focus was on kidney health and related issues. The gin itself was made with "choicest grains" and then flavored with only fresh juniper berries and maple syrup.

Other flavored gins mentioned as sweetened varieties in the Café Royal Cocktail Book included: apricot gin, cherry gin and passion fruit gin. Little is known about them, although suggested recipes can be found in Appendix II.

ORANGE GIN COCKTAILS

Noted authors David Embury, John Doxat and a few more, state that Hollands gin does not tend to mix well and is therefore best consumed on its own. Nonetheless, it was used in a number of examples.

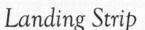

Moulin Rogue

This rose-gold colored drink is the classic orange gin cocktail. Although relatively sweet, the oil from the oranges adds a lively zestiness. The apricot brandy brings out some of the jammy notes of the gin, as does the grenadine. As such, this makes a great alternative to an after dinner liqueur.

3 parts orange gin
1 part apricot brandy
3 dashes of grenadine
Stir

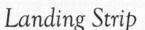

Landing Strip

A Landing Strip is a vibrant cocktail with a slightly malty, woody character. The orange notes are bright and the extra gin balances out the sweetness of the cordial gin, whilst the brandy adds substance and weight to the drink.

Equal parts orange gin, dry gin and brandy
Shake

LEMON GIN COCKTAILS

Windsor Jubilee

Superb, but very tart; this is the sort of drink that wakes you up with a blast of flavor: very fresh, with the tartness neatly balanced by the sweetness of the Cointreau.

2 parts lemon gin
1 part lemon juice
1 part Cointreau
Shake

Gloucester Glory

Complex, with lots of citrus and other fruit notes, making it somewhat reminiscent of a tropical fruit drink. This is one of the fruitiest short gin cocktails out there and although it is a bit involved to mix, it is well worth the effort.

Equal parts apricot brandy, dry vermouth,
lemon gin, lemon juice and orange juice
Shake

APPLE GIN COCKTAILS

There is really only one cocktail of note that calls for apple gin. However, it also works very well in hot toddys and alongside the herbal flavors found in a Martinez.

———◊———

Coronation Cocktail

A superb drink; the dry, sweet, creamy apple notes work exceptionally well with the kirsch (dry), lemon (sour) and orgeat (sweet and creamy). It was smooth, not too sweet, and very fresh.

3 parts apple gin
1 part kirsch
1 part lemon juice
1 part orgeat (almond syrup)
Shake

———◊———

Apple Gin Toddy

A warming drink, with the apple combining nicely with the tart lemon and the spice of the bitters. The sugar contained in the sweet apple gin adds balance.

2 parts sweet apple gin
1 part lemon juice
4 parts boiling water
2 dashes of aromatic bitters
Stir

———◊———

Apple Martinez

Superb, dry apple with a little tannin bitterness and juniper, as well as more complex botanical flavors. These were followed by rich, herbal notes and wormwood, along with the bitterness of the vermouth. This cocktail has a fresh texture that is juicy and invigorating.

2 parts dry apple gin
1 part red vermouth
2 dashes orange bitters
2 dashes maraschino
Shake

MINT COCKTAILS

---•◊•---

Mint Gin Cocktail

This cocktail had a very odd combination of flavors: the dryness of the fortified wines followed after the sweetness of the mint gin. The drink had little synergy and on the whole drink, it was one big clash of flavors. Although this is a good example of a historical cocktail recipe, it is not recommended.

2 parts mint gin
2 parts white port
1 part dry vermouth
Stir the ingredients in a mixing glass with ice and strain into a cocktail glass. Garnish with a fresh sprig of mint.

---•◊•---

Mint Gin Collins

A bracingly fresh and cooling drink: the cool menthol flavors go well with the chilled club soda and ice, and the combination of lemon and mint creates a drink with enough freshness to rival the most elaborate and outrageous of toothpaste commercials.

Equal parts apricot brandy, dry vermouth, lemon gin,
lemon juice and orange juice
Shake

Mint gin also works well as a substitute for dry gin in Martinis, Alexanders and Old Fashioneds.

6

Bitters

Bitters come in two main types: potable and non-potable. Non-potable, aka cocktail bitters, are designed to be consumed in very small quantities–less than 5ml per drink–and are always mixed with other ingredients. Essentially, they are a seasoning for drinks and examples include Angostura and orange bitters. In contrast, potable bitters are designed to be drunk in reasonable quantities, primarily on their own, not necessarily in mixed drinks. Examples include Campari and Suze.

In the early days bitters were often marketed with medicinal properties and so were most likely to be potable, as larger servings were required to obtain the "health benefits". However, in 1912, the US Congress passed the Sherley Amendment, which outlawed false and unproven medical claims. This required various bitters products of the time to rethink their marketing strategies, leading to a greater focus on the cocktail side of their use. This was increased further as people discovered the great difference that just a tiny quantity of these liquids could make to their mixed drinks.

BOKER'S BITTERS

Pronounced either "bowkers" or "bookers" bitters, these aromatic flavor-enhancers were once exceptionally popular and inspired the production of a number of counterfeits. Author and bartender Jerry Thomas advised users of his nineteenth century bar guide to seek out "genuine" Boker's Bitters. Some contemporary authors argue that Bogart's Bitters, another long-lost brand, is simply a corruption of Boker's.

In 1828, John G. Boker created Boker's bitters in New York and it quickly gained favor with the top bartenders of the day. Despite its enduring popularity, American Prohibition quickly caused the company to close. Once the stocks of the bitters were depleted, accurate creations of cocktails such as the East India and the Japanese were impossible.

In 2009, the situation changed when Scottish bitters maker, Dr. Adam Elmegirab, released his version of the bitters, based on a recipe from 1853. His recreation is made using the distinctive cardamom of Boker's, as well as citrus peel and cassia bark. Robert Petrie of Bob's Bitters has also created a batch of Boker's bitters exclusively for the bar at the Dorchester Hotel, which is spicier than Elmegirab's bitters and has a less intensely bitter finish. A third modern day version of Boker's bitters is also being produced by the San Francisco Bitters Company.

ADAM ELMEGIRAB'S BOKER'S BITTERS

NOSE: Thick and intense, with menthol and eucalyptus, cardamom, cassia, citrus (mostly orange) and some lighter, floral notes, such as orris root.

TASTE: Cardamom spice, a touch of orange and then a strong, very long and bitter finish of gentian root.

CELERY BITTERS

Very little is known about celery bitters and few vintage cocktail books call for it in their recipes, so it is perhaps surprising that, today, this obscure ingredient is made by at least three companies. The renewed interest is perhaps due to the intrigue that the unexpected name conjures up, as well as the potential for its use in the classic savory brunch-time cocktails, The Bloody Mary and Red Snapper.

Celery bitters started life as a health tonic, sold to consumers suffering from indigestion, insomnia, headaches and "nervous difficulties." Some vintage bottles also proclaimed that the bitters could add aroma and flavor to almost any liquor and were good for use in cooking.

In 2009, The Bitter Truth released their celery bitters, which went on to win the Spirited Award for "Best New Product" at the 2010 Tales of the Cocktail. The Bitter Truth were inspired by historical research, but since the original had a distinct medicinal focus and there is no record of anyone having tried the celery bitters of old, The Bitter Truth focused on making a product that was suitable for mixing in a twenty-first century bar. Today, Fee Brothers and Scrappy's Bitters also make celery bitters.

THE FLAVOR OF CELERY BITTERS

THE BITTER TRUTH CELERY BITTERS

NOSE: Celery seed and lemon, with hint of verbena, citrus blossom and chocolate.

TASTE: Very fragrant: sweet floral and citrus notes upfront. Gradually, the more complex flavors of the celery seed evolve on the palate, followed by a burst of bitterness and a finish of dry, lightly seasoned, fresh celery.

ABBOTT'S BITTERS

During the golden era of the cocktail, from 1870-Prohibition, there were three brands of cocktail bitters that dominated the USA: aromatic bitters from the House of Angostura produced in Trinidad & Tobago, commonly known as Angostura bitters, Boker's bitters, and Abbott's bitters.

C.W. Abbott's of Baltimore, Maryland, introduced Abbott's bitters in the 1870s and they were quickly adopted by bartenders of the day. Originally, the bitters were called "Abbott's angostura bitters" which indicates they were flavored with angostura bark (*angostura trifoliata*). As Abbott's popularity increased, the company faced legal challenges over their name from the Wupperman Company, the US importer of Angostura bitters (Big "A"), from Trinadad and Tobago. In 1907, Abbott's was forced to drop the word "angostura" from their labels.

It is worth noting here that Angostura bitters do not contain angostura bark, but are instead named after the Venezuelan town of Santo Tomás de Guayana de Angostura del Orinoco, known simply as Angostura. The city is located at the narrows of the Orinoco River and the word "angostura" refers to "narrows" or "narrowness." However, in 1846 the city was renamed Bolivar City. To add to the confusion, angostura bark is named after the same place.

Unlike Boker's bitters, Abbott's bitters managed to survive the Volstead Act in 1920. However, during Prohibition, Abbott's made a change to their label: the man on the label now points at the bottle rather than pouring it, signaling that the bitters were not for recreational consumption. Following the repealing of the 18th Amendment, an additional label was added to the bottleneck stating, "Best for cocktails because it's aged."

Following Prohibition, Abbott's continued to produce its bitters well into the 1950s. The reasons why Abbot's became defunct remains unclear despite it being little more than a half-century ago. Anecdotes tell of commercial problems, changing public tastes, and unpopular reformulations post-prohibition that were weaker in intensity and had a heavy clove-focus. Some writers advocate the (disputed) fact that tonka bean was a key ingredient in their bitters and claim Abbott's ran into trouble when the FDA banned tonka bean in 1954. Other researchers suggest that Abbott's simply lacked profitability. Either way, by the 1960s they were no more.

CONTEMPORARY RECREATIONS OF ABBOTT'S BITTERS

Thirty years after Abbot's went out of business the quest to recreate their bitters began. Interest was reignited in the late 1990s, when a cocktail archaeologist made a version of the bitters, based on an ingredients list from one of the last batches made by Abbott's. The ingredients listed included cassia, cloves, and cardamom. In 2005, Jake Burger and colleagues undertook a gas chromatography–mass spectrometry (GC-MS) analysis on his vintage bottle of Abbott's bitters. The result of this analysis suggested that Abbott's, at one time, contained tonka bean. As of 2013, there are three commercial brands of Abbott's bitters on the market, each with their own back-story recipe and interpretation of what Abbott's would have tasted like.

THE FLAVOR OF ABBOTT'S BITTERS

BOB'S BITTERS

Released in 2011, this was the result of collaboration by various individuals led by Robert Petrie of Bob's Bitters. Their starting point was the results of the GC-MS analysis of Jake Burger's vintage sample.
NOSE: Licorice, gingerbread and a little treacle, followed by basil, orris root and fennel.
TASTE: Rich with hints of Christmas spice, mincemeat and raisin, clove and cinnamon, then a bitter finish with a hint of gum Arabic.

EXTINCT CHEMICAL COMPANY (DARCY O'NEILL)

Released in 2013, this version is based on a recipe that O'Neill found in August 2009 belonging to Joe Abbott. After initially discounting the recipe, O'Neill conducted further research that opened up the possibility of its legitimacy. Interestingly, the recipe contains canella bark—a tree bark that tastes of cinnamon and cloves. In fact, canella is often known as wild cinnamon.
In twenty-first century North America, canella bark is devilishly hard to find and, in the end, O'Neill had to take a field trip to the Caribbean island of Saint Croix in order to harvest a fresh supply. After mixing, the bitters were aged in an ex-whiskey barrel.
NOSE: Black licorice, gingerbread cookie, fennel, basil,

cloves and a hint of perfumed talc.

TASTE: Spice, perfumed cloves and cinnamon. This has a touch of sweetness, followed by notes of anise and dark, sticky black licorice, which transforms into a dark, bitter finish.

TEMPUS FUGIT

Peter Schaf and John Troia of Tempus Fugit Spirits, a company that specializes in vintage-style spirits and liqueurs, were inspired to recreate Abbott's bitters out of their love for collecting antique liquor bottles, especially Abbott's and other bitters bottles. In their quest to recreate the bitters, the duo established a timeline and history of C.W. Abbott's and came across a series of legal documents referring to lawsuits between Abbott's and the American importer of Angostura bitters—the Wupperman company. During the trial, Abbott's claimed that they had the legal right to label their product "Abbott's angostura bitters" because their bitters were flavored with angostura bark.

Schaf and Troia then researched a number of bitters recipes that are based on angostura bark, including some from the estate of bitters marker, O.B. Van Camp. After compiling over twenty recipes, they set about replicating each of them and comparing them with samples extracted from their collection of vintage bottles of Abbott's bitters. The reproductions were then aged in barrels and subjected to micro-oxygenation. This process allowed them to mimic the decades of natural oxidation that their vintage Abbott's experienced, so that they could be compared one-to-one. Finally, they tried their bitters in cocktails. The result of this extensive investigation was their replica of pre-prohibition-style Abbott's bitters.

NOSE: Rich and earthy to start, with notes of licorice, orris root and cassia bark. Softer herbal and floral notes follow sweet anise, violet and intermittent hints of cocoa nibs, with red cinnamon at the end.

TASTE: Rich and aromatic spice, leading onto a bitter finish. To start, notes of cinnamon and cloves, similar to other angostura bark bitters, but with a well balanced flavor—very well-rounded and warming. These have a defined flavor, but are not overpowering, suggesting that they have great mixing potential.

MANHATTAN WITH ABBOTT'S BITTERS

The following tasting notes are on three Manhattan cocktails, each made with a different version of Abbott's bitters. Each Manhattan was made with two parts rye whiskey, one part red vermouth, three dashes of Abbott's, stirred over ice, and strained into a cocktail glass.

BOB'S BITTERS

A spicy drink with sweet, plump flavors. A black cherry garnish would complement it nicely. The character of the whiskey comes through well, accompanied by a hint of chocolate and a touch of cinnamon swirl.

EXTINCT CHEMICAL COMPANY

Some sweetness with anise and an herbal complexity which, together, remind me of absinthe. Given the presence of whiskey in the drink, it brings to mind a Sazerac. All in all, this is a bold cocktail in which the bitters certainly make a difference.

TEMPUS FUGIT

The bitters add some dry spice and a little extra woodiness to the drink, as well as an attractive hint of citrus. There are spicy notes with vanilla and a touch of coconut as well, but the flavors are not too sweet and the bitters complement the interplay between the whiskey and vermouth.

GRAPEFRUIT WITH ABBOT'S BITTERS

Using Abbott's to season half of a grapefruit at breakfast or before dinner has been a long associated use for the product, it is even mentioned on the side of some bottles.

BOB'S BITTERS

Gingerbread spice, giving the fruit a rather festive air. The bitters contrast with the fruit well, complementing its flavors nicely.

EXTINCT CHEMICAL COMPANY

The strong anise, fennel and licorice notes will appeal to fans of these flavors. These bitters add complexity to the flavors of the fruit, making this a good way to spice up the dish without needing to add sugar.

TEMPUS FUGIT

This serve makes a relatively subtle change to the flavors of the fruit, with the bitters acting more as a seasoning, like salt or pepper, rather than a modifier. Delicious.

More cocktail recipes calling for Abbott's bitters can be found in Appendix I.

OTHER BITTERS

STOUGHTON BITTERS

Formulated and patented by Reverend Richard Stoughton in 1712, Stoughton's Elixir was one of the earliest bitters to be called for in cocktail recipes from the nineteenth century. Many household guides and cookbooks from the nineteenth and twentieth centuries contained recipes for these bitters. Stoughton's flavors typically included a heavy bitterness, often provided by gentian root, as well as notes of chamomile and Virginian snakeroot.

KHOOSH BITTERS

Khoosh were a tonic bitters manufactured in the UK by the Khoosh Tonic Bitter Company of Liverpool. They were produced from the early 1880s and were described as being "much used in Woah, India." The bitters were marketed for a dual purpose: medicinal, as a tonic for complaints of the stomach, kidneys and liver; and recreational, for use in wine, mineral waters and spirits; in particular, sherry, gin, brandy and whisky. Contemporary writers doubt that the bitters were ever exported to the US and suggest Khoosh was very bitter and had hints of chiretta herb.

YERBA BUENA

Native to San Francisco, Yerba Buena was a type of herbal bitters produced during the later nineteenth and early twentieth centuries. Businessmen Homer Williams and Alfred Wright first produced them around 1870. Ten years later, Paul O'Burn purchased their company and continued to produce the bitters until Prohibition. The name Yerba Buena comes from an early name for the city of San Francisco. At the center of the flavor of the bitters themselves was a mint that was local to the area; its flavor is similar to spearmint with a hint of oregano.

These three bitters are currently only produced by the San Francisco Bitters Company in California. In addition to these, they make their own version of Boker's, Abbott's, and a host of other vintage bitters.

COCKTAILS
WITH BOKER'S BITTERS

East India Cocktail

This drink is sweet and spicy with a complex finish. The curacao and pineapple syrup add a bright, fruity element to the cocktail and the Boker's bitters add depth and crispness to the finish.

4 parts brandy
1 tsp curacao
1 tsp pineapple syrup
3 dashes of Boker's bitters
2 dashes maraschino
Stir

Japanese

Simply a delicious drink: the orgeat sweetens the brandy and opens up its flavors, including burnt sugar. On top of this, the Boker's bitters add a deep complexity of spice notes.

3 parts brandy
1 part orgeat syrup
2 dashes Boker's bitters
Stir

COCKTAILS
WITH CELERY BITTERS

Cocktails explicitly calling for Celery bitters are rare, but here is one from *The Gentleman's Companion*, published in 1939.

Fourth Regiment
from Commander Livesey

This cocktail is a variation on the Manhattan, but the celery bitters totally transform the finish of the drink. Instead of a bittersweet herbal ending, there are flavors of aromatic celery seed and a note of celery stalk that are so fresh, they are almost crunchy.

2 parts rye whiskey
1 part red vermouth
2 dashes each of celery, orange & Angostura bitters
Stir and garnish with a lime twist.

Celery Gin & Tonic

In the twenty-first century, celery bitters are widely regarded as a seasoning for Gin & Tonics. The bitters add extra flavor to this popular drink, with some anise and a little savory saltiness; rather pleasant and still quite fresh to taste, but with an added level of flavor. The flavors of celery seed and stalk build up as you drink. This works particularly well when using herbal and savory gins, such as Aviation, Gin Mare, Ophir or Darnley's View Spiced.

2 parts gin
2 parts tonic water (Fevertree, Thomas Henry or Q Tonic)
2-3 dashes celery bitters
Stir

Liqueurs

Most cocktails require some sweetness to achieve balance and, when using a liqueur, a whole host of new aromas and flavors can be brought to the drink as well. It is fair to say that liqueurs are the preserve of the most obscure flavors, but also the most difficult to reproduce, whether that product is Forbidden Fruit, Crème Yvette, or Pimento Dram.

CRÈME YVETTE

Crème Yvette, a floral liqueur traditionally flavored with violet petals and other botanicals is, as legend has it, named after French cabaret singer and actress Yvette Guilbert. The Sheffield Company of Connecticut produced Crème Yvette from 1890 until the turn of the twentieth century. The Jacquin Cordial Company of Philadelphia purchased Crème Yvette from Sheffield around that time and produced the cordial until 1969 when they discontinued it due to declining sales.

From then on, cocktails such as the Blue Moon, Angel's Kiss and the Lavender Lady could not be enjoyed in their original formulation. The situation went from bad to worse when Crème Yvette's closest substitute, crème de violette (see page #), was also discontinued.

Crème Yvette returned to the shelves in 2009, when Robert Cooper, creator of St. Germain Elderflower Liqueur, resurrected the Jacquin's family recipe for the liqueur. Unlike its nineteenth and twentieth century predecessor, Cooper now produces Crème Yvette in France. This is partly due to the fact that many of the US suppliers for the original Crème Yvette are no longer in business. Ingredients used to produce the liqueur include: dried violet petals from Provence and Burgundy, as well as blackberries, black currants, raspberries and wild strawberries from the Aquitaine region of France. Cooper makes Crème Yvette with a neutral spirit base, sweetened and packaged in a bottle, based on the shape and style of an original 1940s version.

THE FLAVOR OF CRÈME YVETTE

COOPER SPIRITS' CRÈME YVETTE
COLOR: Rich burgundy
NOSE: Vanilla, strawberries and cream with rose and violet.
TASTE: Crème Yvette has a silky smooth texture, with flavors of sweet violets or violet creams. There are also faint hints of Turkish Delight and purple grape. Sweet and delicious.

CRÈME DE VIOLETTE

Crème de violette (also violet or violettes) and its floral liqueur contemporaries can trace their origins back to Turkey and the Ottomon Empire. The Ottomans did not use distillation to produce alcoholic beverages, but rather made syrups and essences flavored with fruit and flowers. These techniques were picked up by French winemakers who used them to extract flavor with clean alcohol bases and sold them in Syria, India and Africa, where such liqueurs were popular with the locals.

By the eighteenth century, floral liqueurs had made their way back to France, continental Europe, and, eventually, the United States. One of the first offerings of Crème de Violette in the US was sold by a Philadelphian grocer in 1783, along with Eau de Violette, Eau de Celeri and Parfait d'Amour.

In the nineteenth century, crème de violette had become popular with the nobility of Europe and the up-standing families both east and west of the Mississippi. One notable noble who found floral flavors favorable was Alix of Hesse, the wife of Russian Tsar Nicholas II. The Tsarina was said to have used it a great deal, even refusing coffee unless it contained the violet liqueur. At that time, crème de violette was described in one article as a "pure distillation of Russian violets and alcohol base," although many producers created it via maceration.

At the turn of the twentieth century, the popularity of crème de violette and other colorful liqueurs was booming. The USA saw the introduction of Crème Yvette, which was initially described as an American version of the French violette. Other floral liqueurs available at the time included crème de rose, crème de cerise made from cerus flowers, crème de heliotrope, crème de casmin, crème de mille fleurs, and crème de fleur d'orange made from orange blossoms.

All of these liqueurs were used to add a twist to established drinks such as the Fizz, the Rickey and the Daisy. Despite their popularity with the public, who believed that a mere dash would enhance their drink, bartenders and saloon-keepers were less keen, as the liqueurs were quite expensive. Nonetheless, it remained popular. In 1900, a prize was awarded in New Orleans to A.L. Lanata for the best crème de violette. Sixteen years later, the Aviation cocktail–the signature drink for the liqueur—made its first appearance in print.

Unfortunately, the introduction of Prohibition meant that fans of the floral liqueur had to turn to either bootleggers or the legal alternative: non-alcoholic cordials. After a very brief reappearance in the 1930s around the outbreak of World War II, crème de violette once again became difficult to come by, as were many other luxurious liqueurs, and what was available was clearly labeled "Imitation Crème de Violette."

Liqueur sales in general flagged during the 1940s but picked up by the mid-1950s, especially liqueurs that were unusual in color such as the green Crème de Menthe, Parfait d'Amour and–of course–the purple crème de violette. Changing tastes in the 1960s relegated crème de violette to use in novel, multi-colored layered drinks such as the Pousse Café and the Rainbow, which were created in the 1870s. In the UK, things were just as bad. A 1965 episode of the British spy series The Avengers featured the obscurity of crème de violette as a key plot device. But, by 1972, after two centuries of existence, both crème de violette and Crème Yvette disappeared from the market, making it impossible to mix the Pousse Café according to its original recipe.

Crème de violette and, by extension, a true Aviation cocktail, eluded drinkers for over 30 years. This was until the twenty-first century, when Monin, quickly followed by Benoit, began to export their crème de violette outside of France once again. It was not until 2006 that Rothman & Winter began to export their Austrian crème de violette to the USA. In 2009, The Bitter Truth of Germany released their vintage-inspired liqueur, followed by Golden Moon Distillery in 2013.

It is worth noting that changes to the legal definitions of liqueurs introduced in 2008 stipulated a liqueur must contain at least 250g of sugar per liter to be called a crème. As a result, some excellent recreations can no longer use the term on their bottle, even though they adhere to a historically accurate flavor profile for crème de violette.

THE TASTE OF CRÈME DE VIOLETTE

GOLDEN MOON CRÈME DE VIOLETTE
(COURTESY OF AARON KNOLL)

COLOR: A warm translucent purple/pink, redolent of African violet, crocus, rhododendron, or a very dilute concord grape juice and water mix.

NOSE: Floral, hints of dry rose and strawberry against a background of sweet violet. Hints of mixed berry as well.

TASTE: A mild zip initially on the palate; a warming sensation as the liqueur spreads; fresh vibrant violet and an initial sweetness which gently fades as it recedes on the back of the palate, faintly intimating blackberry jam. Finishes with a crisp but mild sweetness, and just a touch of heat in the back of the throat. Nicely balanced, with a restrained sweetness and a clear, but never overpowering floral character.

CRÈME DE ROSÉ

Given the popularity of floral liqueurs such as Crème Yvette and crème de violette, both flavored with violet petals, it is perhaps not surprising that a rose liqueur also exists; namely, crème de rosé. It is still possible to buy rose liqueurs today; Briottet and Courvoisier of France both make them and the Dutch company, Van Wees, produces the curiously-named Rose without Thorns liqueur.

However, none of these are technically crème, as they do not contain sufficient proportions of sugar to be classified as one. There was once a Turkish brand named Gul, which was widely acclaimed, but this has long since disappeared. T.E. Carling described the flavor profile as tasting of "rose petals, citrus and vanilla." One brand of crème de rosé that is available today is Combier, which is produced at a distillery designed by Gustave Eiffel in Saumur, France. Bottled at 25% ABV, it uses a sugar beet base and is produced with both maceration and distillation of rose petals.

A recipe for T.E. Carling's style of liqueur can be found in Appendix II.

THE FLAVOR OF CRÈME DE ROSÉ

T.E. CARLING STYLE CRÈME DE ROSÉ

COLOR: Light rose pink.

NOSE: Plump notes of rose and vanilla, with hints of citrus—indulgent Turkish Delight.

TASTE: Thick, viscous and creamy. As a crème, it is quite sweet and better for mixing or drizzling over desserts then for sipping on its own.

CRÈME DE THÉ

Crème de thé, also known as crème de recco or crème de pekoe, was a tea-based liqueur, typically produced in France. As such, crème de thé would have been produced with a neutral, unaged spirit, probably made from sugar beets. This is still commonly used today in French liqueurs, such as Bénédictine.

Tea is a complex flavor and there are plenty of different blends and varieties available. Additionally, as anyone partial to a cup of tea knows, tea is quick and easy to infuse in liquid. All of these factors make it a great ingredient with which to flavor alcohol.

In the last few years, some new tea liqueurs have been released, but these tend to feature flavors such as green tea and more complex fruit aromas and infusions, rather than focusing on the black teas traditionally used in crème de thé. Marie Brizzard of Burgundy, France, made the most established brand of crème de thé. This started life labeled as a Crème de Thé before being renamed Teabrizz; nowadays, it is simply called Téa. However, this is difficult to come by outside of France.

THE FLAVOR OF CRÈME DE THÉ

MARIE BRIZZARD CRÈME DE THÉ

COLOR: Bright gold.

NOSE: Fragrant black tea and a little orange.

TASTE: Bold, with an initial sweetness, followed by vanilla, orange and the flavor of the tea: fresh black tea leaves. This has a very genuine flavor of the kind that you would expect from a tea liqueur, along with a long, dry finish with a touch of tannin.

PIMENTO DRAM

Pimento dram is a Jamaican rum-based liqueur (bottled around 20-30%ABV) that used to be widely exported and was popular during the American Tiki Cocktail craze. One of its enduring attractions was its versatility and the fact that only a tiny amount was needed to change the flavor profile of a drink. During the 1980s, despite all this, exportation ceased and, until recently, it was only readily available in Jamaica.

Pimento dram is named after the berries of the Pimento tree which is indigenous to the Caribbean; it has nothing to do with the little peppers sometimes stuffed in olives. These berries are also known as Jamaican Pepper or Allspice, because of the resemblance in taste that the dried berries have to a combination of cloves, cinnamon and nutmeg.

In 2009, The Bitter Truth—experts in reviving long-lost ingredients—released their version of a pimento dram. St. Elizabeth of Austria also makes an allspice liqueur, very similar to pimento dram.

THE FLAVOR OF PIMENTO DRAM

THE BITTER TRUTH PIMENTO DRAM

NOSE: Rich, sweet and sticky. Hints of cloves, cinnamon, marzipan, sarsaparilla and strawberry licorice.

TASTE: Soft on the palate, with a fiery cinnamon, clove and the sweetness of root beer. The cinnamon reappears on the finish. It has a sweet flavor, akin to cinnamon balls or Big Red gum.

FORBIDDEN FRUIT

Some long-lost ingredients are noteworthy because of their underlying concept, i.e. their flavor or ingredients, whilst others are known for their prevalence in vintage cocktail books. There is one liqueur, however, that fascinates because of its ornate bottle and provocative name: Forbidden Fruit. T.E. Carling described it as being "flame colored grapefruit and orange," whilst other authors from decades past focused on its grape brandy base spirit, high alcoholic strength and bitter aftertaste. However, not all twentieth century authors were complimentary to the liqueur. David Embury placed it in his bottom two spirits along with the perfumed Parfait d'Amour.

While the Bustanoby family of New York invented and owned Forbidden Fruit, the Joseph Krieg Fink Company of New Jersey made it until WW1. The name comes from an early moniker for the grapefruit, a Bermuda-born natural cross between the shaddock (pomelo) and sweet orange citrus fruits. The grapefruit was introduced in Florida around 1823 with the first shipments to New York and Philadelphia in 1885.

The distinctive bottle was designed to resemble the Orb of Charles II and was patented by André Bustanoby in February 1904. The bottle was originally topped with a cross pattée, also known as a Maltese cross, but around the outbreak of World War I, the Bustanoby family changed it to a crown.

The Bustanoby's had some success with the liqueur and they served it in their Manhattan restaurant/bar, Café des Beaux Arts, located at 40th Street and 6th Avenue. A 1917 newspaper article described the bar in great detail; this was a "bar for women," which meant that only women were allowed to order and a man could only drink there if he was chaperoned by a lady. Cocktails from that article can be found in Appendix I. The clientele of Café des Beaux Arts' bar were known to have had a sophisticated palette and Bustanoby even redesigned the shape of his brandy glasses from the traditional balloon to a style more similar to the modern tulip glass to appeal to their sophistication.

By 1934, the Jacquin Liqueur Company, makers of Rock & Rye, grenadine, apricot brandy, crème de menthe, blackberry brandy and a raspberry liqueur named Chambord, purchased Forbidden Fruit. When the Bustanoby's sold Forbidden Fruit, they also sold the patent for their bottle design. Jacquin adopted the design for Chambord and some of their other products. Chambord continued to be packaged in the Forbidden Fruit-style bottle, until a recent redesign a few years ago. Shortly after the sale, Jacquin swapped the traditional Forbidden Fruit bottle for a more basic orb bottle and, by December 1974, it was sold in a plain, long-necked bottle.

In 1951, the alcoholic strength of Forbidden Fruit dropped from the original 40% ABV to 35% ABV. A 1905 advertisement described Forbidden Fruit as "a blend of Grape Fruit juice and Old Cognac Fine Champagne." By the mid-1960s the description changed to "made of imported Valencia oranges, honey and fine brandy," indicating a likely recipe change. In the mid-1970s, along with changes in the bottle shape, the ABV of Forbidden Fruit dropped once again to 32% and, in the early 1980s, it was discontinued completely.

The story of Forbidden Fruit picked up again in 2011 when the Dorchester Hotel in London was preparing to celebrate their 80th anniversary and wanted a signature celebration cocktail for the bar. A natural candidate was the Dorchester of London, taken from the 1951 book Bottom's Up, a drink which author Ted Saucier credits to: "Harry Craddock American Bar, The Dorchester, London." The cocktail, Dorchester of London, is a combination of Bacardi white rum, dry gin and Forbidden Fruit. But, with no commercial varieties of the liqueur being produced, the bar turned to the then Dorchester's pastry chef, Robert Petrie, aka Bob of Bob's Bitters, for help.

After extensive research, Bob formulated an idea of how to recreate Forbidden Fruit and his product was finished in time for the anniversary event. For the same event, Giuliano Morandin, head bartender of The Bar at The Dorchester Hotel, had managed to acquire an original bottle of Forbidden Fruit. For the first time, both could be tasted side-by-side, with pleasing results.

[Liqueurs]

No. 36,764.

DESIGN

PATENTED FEB. 2, 1904.

A. BUSTANOBY.
BOTTLE.
APPLICATION FILED JAN. 6 1904.

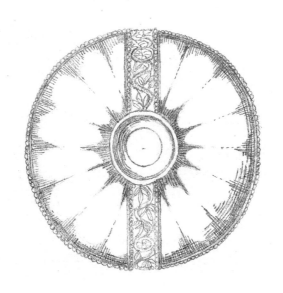

THE FLAVOR OF FORBIDDEN FRUIT

A recent tasting of four different bottles of Forbidden Fruit at the Dorchester's bar had the following results:

....

BOB'S BITTERS RECREATION–CIRCA 2011

One of the most notable aspects of the descriptions of Forbidden Fruit is the flame-like color, and the rich tones of yellow, amber, and red in this recreation captures this well. The richness continues to the nose, with orange grapefruit and a hint of honey. Flavorwise, there is a citrus freshness that is followed by a sweet, honey middle and then a dark, bitter finish.

Vintage Bottle I–Circa 1930s

This is slightly darker in color than the recreation and the age of the spirit comes through on the nose. When tasted against the Dorchester's recreation, the similarity is uncanny; the vintage version is perhaps a little earthier and bitter, but this is to be expected from a spirit that is over half a century old. The combination of initial sweetness and following bitterness of Forbidden Fruit is unlike any other liqueur.

Vintage Bottle II–Circa 1940s

This version is an even darker color than the other vintage sample. The nose is of intense, earthy citrus, before the grapefruit-like character comes through. The flavor is similarly intense, with a lot of bitterness, slightly reminiscent of China Martini or some other quinquina liqueurs. There is also lots of citrus, some gentian and dry cinnamon bark. Only a small amount would be needed for a drink.

Vintage Bottle III - Circa 1960s

Notably lighter in color than all of the previous samples, this has a stickier nose and a more viscous texture, with hints of maple and pancake syrup. The taste is very sweet with only a slight, dry bitterness at the end. It hasn't aged as well as the others; there are very little citrus or any other confectionary notes, and the finish is certainly that of pancake syrup, just like the one that they have at McDonalds.

PIMM'S & OTHER FRUIT CUPS

Fruit cups, a mix of spirit, wine and liqueurs, have never really left the market, and Pimm's No. 1–the poster child for fruit cups—has been continually produced for over 170 years. In the 1960s, there were six varieties of Pimm's, each made with a different spirit base. Gin is the base for the original fruit cup, hence bearing the number 1. Pimm's No.1 Cup was originally released in 1840. Following the success of No.1, Samuel Moray introduced Pimm's No.2 Cup in 1851, which had a Scotch whisky base. Also launched in 1851, Pimm's No.3 Cup was a fruit cup based on brandy. In 2005, Diageo released a variation of No.3 called Winter Pimm's that had a brandy base with spices and orange peel.

Introduced in 1933, Pimm's No.4 Cup was based on dark rum. It was created so that it could be served both hot and cold. As a historical side note, Julius Wile & Sons, the one-time US importer of Pimm's, used a blend of rum and brandy for their version of No.4 and it seems likely that this was for reasons of logistics rather than taste.

In the 1960s, Pimm's' parent company introduced two new fruit cups. Pimm's No.5 Cup, originally produced for the Canadian market, had a base of Canadian rye whisky. Following its success in Canada, No.5 was introduced to the UK and US in 1964. Also introduced in 1964, Pimm's No.6 Cup has a vodka base and a lighter, less herbal character than the gin-based No.1.

Cups 1 through 6 continued to be produced until 1970, when Pimm's was sold to The Distiller's Company, which later became part of Diageo. Due to reduced demand for No.2 through No.6, The Distiller's Company discontinued them in a bid to focus on sales of the bestselling No.1 Cup. However, the No.6 vodka cup only ceased production for a period of three weeks before being brought back. The reason? It was a favorite of the chairman's wife. Recently, in 2013, Diageo released Pimm's Blackberry & Elderflower, based on the Pimm's No.6 vodka cup. This flavored fruit cup is a seasonal supplement to their original gin-based cup. In Summer 2014, Diageo announced that the Pimm's No.6 cup would, for commercial reasons, cease to be produced, ending a run of over fifty years, minus those three weeks, of course.

Today, gin, brandy and vodka-based fruit cups are available from a number of manufacturers other than Pimm's, but there are currently no scotch, rye or rum fruit cups made by any company. The strength of fruit cups range from 20-30% ABV and there are a plethora of spirits which can be used as a base for the drink.

THE FLAVORS OF FRUIT CUPS

When designing a fruit cup for a particular spirit, it is useful to reflect upon how the drink is usually mixed and take the flavors from those cocktails to inspire the character of your fruit cup. Also worth considering is whether to look at a particularly seasonal recipe.

A BASIC FORMULA FOR FRUIT CUP

BASE SPIRIT	+	SWEET	+	VERMOUTH	+	CITRUS PEEL	+	INFUSION

FOR EXAMPLE

Gin, brandy, whisk(e)y, or tequila	+	Ginger wine, orange liqueur, or other liqueur	+	Sweet vermouth, dry vermouth, amaro, or other fortified wines	+		+	Spices, herbs, or berries

Here are some recommended fruit cup combination to inspiration your own creativity.

SPIRIT BASE	SUGGESTED SEASONALITY	SUGGESTED FLAVORS
Absinthe	Spring/Summer	Lemon, basil, sage, lemon thyme
Cachaça	Summer	Pink grapefruit, vanilla
Cachaça	Winter	Lime, cinnamon, clove
Calvados	Autumn	Orange, cinnamon, ginger
Dark Rum	All-year	Lime, all-spice, pimento dram, dark sugar
Irish Whiskey	Spring	Rhubarb, lemon
Islay Scotch	Autumn	Blueberry, cranberry, ginger
Poteen/Poitin	Summer	Dry vermouth, lemon, grapefruit
Scotch Whisky	Autumn/Winter	Orange, ginger, honey, spice
Soju	Spring/Summer	Green tea, persimmon
Tequila	Summer	Lime, orange
White Whiskey	All-year	Marmalade

Specific recipes for Scotch, Tequila and Soju-based fruit cups can be found in Appendix II.

MIXING AND GARNISHING FRUIT CUPS

Fruits cups are not typically used in cocktails; instead, they are "prepared," which involves adding a soft drink to lengthen the cup and an appropriate garnish. In the UK, lemon lime sodas, such as Sprite or 7UP, are traditionally used and work quite well. Fruit cups are also sometimes mixed with tonic, ginger ale, bitter lemon or ginger beer. For an alternative to sparkling drinks, you could try using homemade lemonade or unsweetened iced tea.

There are a few other factors to consider. When mixing a fruit cup at a strength of 25-30% ABV, a ratio of one part cup to three parts mixer is a good starting place but, in practice, it all depends upon the relative intensity of flavors of the cup and the mixer to be used. In the summer months, ice is a necessity and for warm winter fruit cups, it is wise to use hot tea or warm fruit juice as a mixer rather than heating a carbonated drink, as the bubbles can become a little harsh.

Garnishes are another important aspect of serving fruit cups. Pimm's was traditionally garnished with lemon and borage but, today, lime, orange, mint and cucumber are all valid options. The seasonality and spirit base of a fruit cup are perfect for inspiring garnish choices, helping to make a drink that is both tasty and visually engaging.

OTHER LIQUEURS

CRÈME DE GENIÈVE

This was a juniper-flavored liqueur that consisted of a juniper distillate (i.e. a single botanical gin) that had been matured in casks for a period of 4-6 weeks and then sweetened with sugar. Although popular in the late nineteenth century, no crème de genièves are currently produced. Hayman's of England make a Gin Liqueur, although this contains other botanical flavors in addition to juniper, and it is not matured in wood.

COCONUT WHISQUEUR

A rather unlikely sounding liqueur, Coconut Whisqueur had a Scotch whisky base that was flavored with coconut. It was produced in the 1960s and 70s, and was also a popular filling for liqueur chocolates. In 2006, Berry Bros and Rudd released a similar product for the Puerto Rican Market. Cutty Coco is a coconut liqueur blended with Cutty Sark Scotch Whisky, the bestselling whisky on the island. Bottled at 24% ABV, it is blended and bottled in Puerto Rico and was inspired by the local custom of drinking Scotch with coconut water.

A recipe for Coconut Whisquer can be found in Appendix II.

FIVE FRUITS AND SEVEN FRUITS LIQUEURS

These are a little-known set of Italian liqueurs, flavored with five and seven different citrus fruits, respectively. Some citrus fruits included in the recipe are lemon, lime, orange, mandarins, chinottos and citrons. Before US Prohibition, Julius Marcus of Detroit, Michigan, made an "all natural" seven fruits liqueur and equivalent, non-alcoholic syrup. The fruits mentioned on their labels included lemons, oranges, pineapple, strawberries, raspberries, cherries and plums. However, a number of investigations in the early 1930s by the US Government determined that these fruit liqueurs were artificially flavored and thus misleading. After this investigation, they were discontinued. Today, the only producer of a Seven Fruits Liqueur is Mangilli, a small Italian firm from Udine, that produces a bottling at 18% ABV.

COCKTAILS
WITH CRÉME YVETTE

NY Flyer

This is a variation on the Aviation, where gin is replaced by rye whiskey and the crème de violette with Crème Yvette. The result is a drink that is tart, but with warmth and sweetness from the rye, which is complemented by the floral and berry notes of the Yvette. This is a bold and less flowery drink than the Aviation.

4 parts rye whiskey
3 parts lemon juice
2 parts Créme Yvette
1 part maraschino
Shake

Blue Moon

Floral and anise flavors, despite the lack of any absinthe, with a little citrus and violet. Considering that the drink only contains two ingredients, this is a rather complex cocktail with excellent, elegant flavors.

4 parts dry gin
1 part Créme Yvette
Stir and garnish with a lemon twist.

Lavender Lady

There is an exceptional balance of the various ingredients: sweet floral notes, with hints of apples to start, then the citrus of the orange and lemon. The bitterness of the gin follows, along with the warmth of the calvados. The finish is full of flavors of apples and strawberries.

4 parts dry gin
1 part Créme Yvette
Stir and garnish with a lemon twist.

COCKTAILS
WITH CRÉME DE VIOLETTE

———•◊•———

Aviation

The signature cocktail of crème de violette actually uses only a dash or two of the liqueur but it certainly makes a difference. Hugo Ensslin, who was head bartender at the Hotel Wallick in New York City, first published the Aviation in the 1916 book, Recipes for Mixed Drinks. For the decades when violette was not available, parfait d'amour was sometimes used or, otherwise, the Maraschino was dialed up a bit.

2 parts dry gin
1 part lemon juice
2 dashes maraschino
2 dashes Créme de Violette
Shake

———•◊•———

Blue Moon

Floral and anise flavors, despite the lack of any absinthe, with a little citrus and violet. Considering that the drink only contains two ingredients, this is a rather complex cocktail with excellent, elegant flavors.

4 parts dry gin
1 part Créme Yvette
Stir and garnish with a lemon twist.

COLOR: Rose, slight purple pink
tint. Subtle.
NOSE: Fresh lemon and candies,
violet, fragrant.
TASTE: At first, fresh lemon
dominates, but in the middle, cherry
blossom. Finished with fresh violets,
lilac and berry; hint of earth–intensely
flavorful with a long citrus aftertaste.

COCKTAILS
WITH CRÉME DE ROSÉ

Crescent Moon

Dry, tart flavors, somewhat reminiscent of a Gin Collins garnished with the floral indulgence of the rose. Light and refreshing, this could be called a Garden Collins and would work well with gins such as Miller's or Hendricks.

1 part dry gin
1 part Créme de Rosé
1 part lemon juice
Add ice to a highball glass and top up with club soda.

Vicomte Cocktail

Similar to a Wet Martini but with some sweet floral notes, although the overall effect is quite subtle. This is a good choice for those who find an after dinner liqueur too sweet.

4 parts dry gin
3 parts Créme de Rosé
3 parts dry vermouth
Shake

Alexandretta

A light pink hue, with a nose of sweet rose. Creamy and indulgent, this has hints of vanilla, Turkish Delight and then a touch of dry juniper and citrus at the end. Rich and fragrant, but not sweet and sickly.

3 parts dry gin
2 parts Créme de Rosé
2 parts fresh cream
Shake

COCKTAILS
WITH CRÉME DE THÉ

Assam

The classic flavors of the Manhattan are followed by the dry, tea tannin on the finish. This is a drink with elements of both the sweet and dry Manhattan. Perfect.

4 parts rye whiskey
2 parts red vermouth
1 part Créme de Thé
3 dashes orange bitters
Stir

Rosie

Fresh, crisp, dry and refreshing, much like alcoholic iced tea. This is a good variation on the White Lady that allows the crème de thé to shine through.

4 parts gin
1 part Créme de Thé
1 part Triple Sec
2 parts lemon juice
Shake

English High Tea

This tastes like a cross between an ice tea and a Gin Collins: crisp, with the refreshment of tea, zest of citrus and powerful complexity of gin.

1 part gin
1 part Créme de Thé
1 part lemon juice
4 parts soda water

COCKTAILS
WITH PIMENTO DRAM

Lion's Tail

The classic pimento dram cocktail, this has a predominant flavor of bourbon, but with a little added sharpness from the lime and a sweet spiciness from the dram. It is, however, very balanced and is a good way to enjoy the pimento dram playing a subtle part in a cocktail.

4 parts bourbon
1 part Pimento Dram
1 part lime juice
1 tsp. of sugar syrup
1 dash Angostora bitters
Shake

Almost Rye

Reminiscent of an Old Fashioned cocktail, this drink is dominated by the pimento dram, which adds slight sweetness and powerful spice to the whiskey which, in turn, provides an alcoholic backbone to the drink and stops it from becoming sickly.

5 parts rye whiskey
1 part Pimento Dram
Stir and garnish with a lemon twist.

Mayfair

The jamminess of the apricot brandy goes well alongside the sweet spiciness of the dram, whilst the orange gives the drink freshness, and the gin is a suitably subtle base spirit. This drink is really about the other ingredients, not the gin, and so works best with a classic-style dry gin.

6 parts dry gin
2 parts apricot brandy
2 parts fresh orange juice
1 part Pimento Dram
Shake

COCKTAILS
WITH FORBIDDEN FRUIT

The Dorchester

A dry flavor to start, followed by a creamy sweetness and then the bitter-sweet citrus of the liqueur. The notes of the gin and rum frame the liqueur well and are a showcase for its flavors.

4 parts dry gin
2 parts Bacardi white rum
2 parts Forbidden Fruit

Adam & Eve Cocktail

A tart drink with lots of power behind it and full of the character of the Forbidden Fruit: sweet orange to start, then bitter citrus comes through at the end.

Equal parts dry gin, cognac, Forbidden Fruit
a dash of lemon juice
Shake

Tantalus
by *Jack Bushby of the Cecil Bar, Paris*

The warming notes of the brandy, honey and citrus give this drink the feel of a toddy. It is rich, with a good balance of tart and bittersweet flavors, thanks to the Forbidden Fruit.

Equal parts brandy, Forbidden Fruit, lemon juice.

Interviews

STEPHAN BERG / THE BITTER TRUTH

Stephen Berg, along with Alexander Hauck, founded The Bitter Truth in Germany in 2006. They make a variety of bitters, liqueurs and other specialty spirits, which are recreations or inspired by historical products.

SMITH: **What sparked your initial interest in old recipes and forgotten cocktail ingredients?**
BERG: We were fascinated by the whole concept of working in a bar, making drinks and, of course, enjoying drinks ourselves; and the more we got into the scene, the more fascinated we were. So, with all the internet, blogs and forums—mostly Drinkboy at that time—I was deep into classic cocktails. I worked in one of the real classic bars in Munich and started collecting old recipe books and bitters. Back in the day, Germany was pretty much a white spot for new product releases and the spirits and bar market was pretty poor so, at some point, it got me thinking and I thought that if I wanted bitters, I would have to make my own, which then led to The Bitter Truth, once I met Alexander Hauck.

SMITH: **How do you balance your desire to recreate a long-lost cocktail ingredient in an accurate style with your desire to add your own creativity and interpretation to the product?**
BERG: We generally use the past as a base and develop things to meet with today's demands. We are wise enough to realize that the past wasn't always better, that consumer tastes change over time and that modern times may require some aspects in the creations that weren't required a hundred years ago. We always follow the route that we create a product for ourselves first and, once we like it, we're pretty much on the right track. Celery bitters is a good example for that. In the old days, it was some kind of medicine taken to enhance maleness, but as nobody we know has tried old celery bitters, we were free to create a product that would find use on today's bar shelves. One must also realize that a vast number of products disappeared simply because they were not favored by consumers and, looking back, they get mystified.

SMITH: **You are known for your fine selection of bitters and this is a market that has certainly been growing over the last five years. Where do you think it will be in another ten?**
BERG: We think the bitters craziness we have seen in the last couple of years will calm down a bit to a reasonable level. You can hardly surprise anybody with some new bitters now unless it is pretty outstanding. When we started, there was almost nothing available and we did the right thing at the right time. In recent years, we saw products released that sometimes would hardly deserve the name bitters. For a while, you could call anything a "bitters" and people would buy it without even asking what it is. This will come to an end, simply because there may be no bar space left to add the twentieth bottle of bitters. Those brands and flavors that really add something distinctive to a cocktail will remain.

Smith: Which countries do you think are particularly interested in long-lost spirits?

Berg: Definitely the USA and UK, but more or less all countries with a sort of cocktail culture. The last few years have brought a tremendous number of products back to our shelves and today's bartenders have almost everything they need. There are very few white spots left, and now's the time to see which ones will stand the test of time. We can just imagine how bartenders in 50 or 100 years will look into lost spirits, as we live in times where one could fill books with products that are discontinued due to too little success in the market.

Smith: Is there a product not currently on the market that you would like to see?

Berg: Well, maybe some excellently crafted Creme Noyeaux or aged peach brandy.

Smith: What is your favorite way to enjoy one of your products?

Berg: We're classic cocktail drinkers, so we love Dry Martinis, Manhattans, and the like. Nothing fancy. A Gin & Tonic made with our Pink Gin always rocks the boat.

ERIK ELLESTAD / SAVOY STOMP

Erik Ellestad of Savoy Stomp—a website that features each cocktail from the original Savoy Cocktail Book individually, as well as the obscure ingredients that the recipes sometimes call for.

Smith: How did you first get interested in long-lost cocktail ingredients?

Ellestad: In 2006, I volunteered as the moderator of a cocktails and spirits forum. I was looking for a good way to learn about cocktails, short of getting a job at a bar. I thought maybe I'd make all of the cocktails from a book; I wanted to learn about the flavor palate of traditional cocktails. The Savoy Stomp documents my tasting and mixing my way through the cocktails of *The Savoy Cocktail Book.*

Smith: 2006 was quite a different time in terms of the availability of some of these ingredients. Old Tom gin hadn't even come back then. How different was that to today?

Ellestad: Well, absinthe was still illegal in the US and it was difficult to find apricot liqueur and real sloe gin. Vermouth hadn't gone through its revival, so I had to make a lot more from scratch. I made everything from apricot liqueur to plum-infused gin. My first bottle of crème de violette came from a friend returning from a vacation in London. When it comes to lost ingredients, I think about them in three categories:

1) No one makes the ingredient anymore, anywhere;

2) The ingredient is not available where you are; and

3) The ingredient is still made, but the manufacturers have significantly changed its flavor character.

Smith: Which revived ingredient makes the biggest difference to a drink?

Ellestad: Absinthe in the US has had the biggest impact and maybe also apricot liqueur. It's nice that some bars, especially in and around San Francisco, have used my recipe for Hercules in their bar.

Smith: What would you like to see made commercially that isn't currently?

Ellestad: I think I'm less interested in historical recreations now than I am in products that capture local flavors, like bitters with flavors that are associated with the geographical area that you are in. A good quality Amer Picon would also be a good drink, and fruit cups are pretty cool, because we don't really get them in the US.

Smith: You're known for your research into the very obscure ingredient, Hercules. Can you share some of your knowledge?

ELLESTAD: It's required for a drink (Angler Cocktail) that is featured early on in The Savoy Cocktail Book. My initial information came from the Cocktail DB website which, in turn, came from the Stan Jones Complete Bar Guide, which states that *Hercules* is a substitute for absinthe.

As a result, we are all sure that the drinks containing Hercules were absinthe cocktails, but I started making them with absinthe and they weren't drinkable. One day, I looked at an advert for an aperitif titled Hercules. I then found other adverts from the early twentieth century, describing it as an aperitif wine flavored with Yerba Mate. I researched potential recipes using Yerba Mate, on which I based my Hercules, along with some experimentation. However, we still don't know the exact flavors of the spices.

STEPHEN GOULD / GOLDEN MOON DISTILLERY

Stephen Gould is the founder and master distiller at Maison de le Vie in Golden, Colorado, near Denver. They make absinthe, gin, apple brandy, grappa and a host of other liqueurs and specialty spirits.

SMITH   **What inspired your interest in long-lost liquors?**
GOULD: I worked in a restaurant as saucier, then as a sommelier and a bartender. I then started to buy old wine collections and old bottles of booze–just for fun–from estate sales. I'd buy old bottles for $5 apiece, sight unseen. It was like drinking history—every bottle was an adventure.

I came across a case of mid twentieth century absinthe which came from Spain, and I really enjoyed drinking it; it was much better than the Bohemian absinthe I had had in Prague. Two weeks later, I came across an old French book on distilling that contained a collection of absinthe recipes. I thought to myself, in my naivety, "I used to be brewer; I've done some distilling; I know how to work with herbs; I can make this stuff." In reality, I couldn't, but I can now.

SMITH: **What was the first item in your book collection?**
GOULD: A 1851 edition of *Nouveau Manuel Complet du Distillateur et du Liquoriste*. This started me on a quest to build a large research library, mostly for my own use, but I do now let distillers come and use the collection. It now covers over 500 titles from the 1500s to modern books, but most are from the 1800s. I also have a small collection of handwritten distillers' notebooks.

SMITH: **What is the most recent addition to your collection?**
GOULD: A pristine copy of Jacques-François Demachy's *L'art du Distillateur d'eaux-fortes, du Distillateur Liquoriste from 1773*. It is what George Washington ordered from France; he waited one and half years to get the book before opening his distillery at Mount Vernon. The stills in his distillery were built by Coppersmith and based on designs in the back of the book–exciting for any American distiller.

SMITH: **You're well known for your excellent crème de violette. Can you speak a little about that?**
GOULD: Violette liqueurs have always fascinated me, as they are key ingredients in so many classic cocktails. I started mine by researching how they were put together. Violet is a very fragile flavor to work with. Nineteenth century French perfumers would put the flowers into wooden frames with beeswax-covered silk stretched across them. They would put flowers onto that and let the wax soak into the flowers before distilling the violet-infused wax.

This showed that using standard distillation would be difficult. Historically, and today, the bulk of crème de violette is not made by distillation, but maceration; essentially, they are sweetened tinctures. My solution was to use a lot of violet, not just the petals, and also use some other botanicals to stabilize the extraction of violet oil. The other botanicals add some hints of flavor, as well as a natural, creamy note; and so, we can use less sugar. Unlike other distillers, we also use organic grape extract color, unlike other distillers, the result being a higher quality, true violette product.

[Interviews]

SMITH: In addition to the absinthe and the violette, are there any other ingredients you have resurrected?

GOULD: I grew up in Northern Nevada and we have the largest Basque community outside of the Basque region. Picon Punch (brandy, Amer Picon and grenadine) is a natural drink of the Basque region; it's popular there and it's one of my favorite cocktails of all of them.

Original Amer Picon is very bitter—dry orange and cinchona—an amaro liqueur, but the modern version is sweeter and has a lower ABV. It has a different flavor: more orange, less cinchona, sweeter, less hot and less pepper. As such, I started looking into making an Amer Picon in the original style. I happened to purchase a collection of handwritten distillers' notebooks from a woman in Provence, France. I was initially only interested in her grandfather's unique absinthe recipes, but when I looked through, I found a few pages with the heading "Phillipsburg 1851" (where Amer Picon had a distillery) and, lo and behold, they were these distiller's handwritten notes on how to make what seemed to be Amer Picon.

Amer Picon was created in 1839 by Gaetan Picon as a tonic to treat his own malaria symptoms, which he contracted while serving in the French Army in North Africa. One of the key ingredients was cinchona bark, and this was the first commercial anti-malarial drug, even pre-dating commercial tonic water.

Our Amer Dit Picon—which translates as "Amer the way Picon should be"—is bottled at 39% ABV and is a close facsimile of Amer Picon circa 1850. It makes an absolutely wonderful Brooklyn Cocktail and an amazing Picon Punch.

SMITH: Who do you admire for their work in long-lost spirits?

GOULD: David Nathan Maister—Oxygenee, UK. He's written a number of books on rare spirits and is reviving several defunct distilleries from the 1800s, along with their products. He's recreating a cherry liqueur that has not been seen since the early 1900s, using the original cherry orchard and the original stills in the original distillery.

Juan Garza—Tuthilltown Spirits. Very much a kindred spirit and, like David, he takes the approach of not only recreating the spirit, but recreating the manufacturing process that allows the spirit to have that unique flavor.

SMITH: What is your favorite way to drink one of your products?

GOULD: I like to taste what a distiller has created, so I tend to drink them straight. But I also like to experiment with cocktails of the period that the ingredient came from: Absinthe Drip, Sazerac, Wink (Gin Sazerac), and my favorite this week, the Golden Eagle.

The Golden Eagle

3 parts Golden Moon Gin
1 part violette
juice of half a lemon
1 tsp sugar
1 egg white
SHAKE once without ice,
SHAKE a second time with ice to chill and STRAIN.

OLD TOM GIN

Astoria

2 parts dry vermouth
1 part Old Tom gin
2 dashes orange bitters
STIR

Casino Cocktail

6 parts Old Tom gin
2 dashes maraschino
2 dashes orange bitters
2 dashes lemon juice
STIR–cherry

The Defender

3 parts Old Tom gin
3 parts red vermouth
1 part Crème Yvette
dash of orange bitters
STIR

Gin Cocktail

4 parts Old Tom gin
1 dash orange bitters
STIR

Gin Fizz

6 parts Old Tom gin
3 dashes lemon juice
1 teaspoonful powdered sugar
SHAKE–top up with club soda

Improved Tom Gin Cocktail

3 parts Old Tom gin
1 dash curaçao
2 dashes bitters
STIR

Martinez Cocktail

1 part Old Tom gin
1 part red vermouth
2 dashes orange bitters
1 dash syrup
STIR–cherry

Martini Cocktail (Sweet)

2 parts Old Tom gin
1 part red vermouth
2 dashes gum syrup
1 dash orange bitters
STIR

Gordon's
Special
OLD TOM GIN
For those who prefer a slightly sweetened gin
DISTILLED IN LONDON
ENGLAND
GORDON'S
SPECIAL
OLD TOM
SPECIAL
QUALITY
THIS GIN IS SPECIALLY PREPARED FOR THOSE WHO PREFER A SLIGHTLY SWEETENED GIN AND THE NAME
GORDON'S
EMBODIES THE VERY HIGHEST STANDARDS OF QUALITY AND

Pre-Prohibition Martini

2 parts Old Tom gin
2 parts red vermouth
dash orange bitters
STIR–olive

Princess Marina

Equal parts:
Old Tom gin
peach brandy
Lillet Blanc
SHAKE

Princeton Cocktail

6 parts Old Tom gin
2 dashes of orange bitters
1 teaspoon port wine
SHAKE–lemon twist

Rickey

3 parts Old Tom gin
2 parts lime juice
6 parts club soda
Pour ingredients
into a tall glass with ice

St. Francis Special Martini

3 parts Old Tom gin
1 part dry vermouth
STIR –lemon twist

Tom Collins

6 parts Old Tom gin
4 parts lemon juice
2 parts sugar syrup
10 parts club soda
STIR

Tom Gin Cocktail

6 parts Old Tom gin
1 part sugar syrup
2 dashes orange bitters
STIR– lemon twist

Tuxedo Cocktail

8 parts Old Tom gin
8 parts French vermouth
2 dashes orange bitters
1 dash maraschino
1 dash absinthe
STIR–lemon twist
and cherry navy gin

YELLOW GIN

Blue Lady

2 parts yellow gin
1 part blue curaçao
1 part lemon juice
Dash of egg white
SHAKE

Bristolian

Equal Parts:
yellow gin
Lillet Blanc
Aurum
Gran Marnier
STIR–orange peel twist

Bullseye

2 parts yellow gin
2 parts ginger liqueur
1 part lemon juice
1 part orange juice
SHAKE

Crest Club–St. Moritz

4 parts yellow gin
3 parts grapefruit juice
2 parts Grand Marnier
SHAKE

Darlington

4 parts yellow gin
2 parts dry vermouth
2 parts lemon juice
1 part blue curaçao
1 part Calvados
dash of gum syrup
SHAKE

Dee Don

3 parts yellow gin
3 parts Lillet Blanc
1 part dry pash
1 part Benedictine
SHAKE

Georgia

2 parts yellow gin
2 parts lemon juice
1 part Strega liqueur
1 part sugar syrup
SHAKE

Golfers Special

2 parts yellow gin
2 parts cherry brandy
1 part Lillet Blanc
1 part lemon juice
dash of orange bitters
SHAKE

Goody-goody

4 parts yellow gin
2 parts Dubonet Red
1 part lemon juice
1 part Yellow Chartreuse
SHAKE

Inky's Special

2 parts yellow gin
2 parts lime juice
dash of kummel
dash of anisette
SHAKE

Jubilant

4 parts yellow gin
2 parts Benedictine
1 part lemon juice
1 part orange juice
egg whites
SHAKE

Le Canadien

Equal parts
yellow gin
Cointreau
orange juice
3 dashes grenadine
SHAKE

Floating Power

2 parts orange curaçao
1 part yellow gin
1 part lemon juice
dash of rum and egg white
SHAKE

Life Blood Warmer

2 parts yellow gin
1 part Cointreau
1 part lemon barley water
1 part orange juice
SHAKE

Pickwell Manor

Equal parts:
yellow gin
cognac
Grand Marnier
unsweetened pineapple juice
SHAKE

The Stanhope

4 parts yellow gin
2 parts apricot brandy
1 part orange juice
1 part passion fruit juice
1 dash peach bitters
SHAKE

New Waldorf

2 parts yellow gin
1 part dry vermouth
1 part red vermouth
quarter slice of pineapple (crushed)
SHAKE

HOLLANDS GIN

Absinthe Continental

Rinse a cocktail glass with absinthe
add Hollands gin and ice
STIR

Dog's Nose

3 parts Hollands gin
12 parts pale lager (Belgium style)

The Duchy's Original

6 parts Hollands gin
1 part sugar syrup
3 dashes Abbott's or other
angostura bark
bitters
STIR

Fantasio Cocktail

2 parts Hollands gin
2 parts brandy
1 part white crème de menthe
1 part maraschino

John Collins

2 parts Hollands gin
1 part fresh lemon juice
1 part sugar syrup
6 parts club soda
STIR

Low Martini

4 parts Hollands gin
2 parts Red vermouth
2 dashes Abbott's bitters
STIR –orange twist

Marengo

2 parts Hollands gin
6 parts ginger ale
dash of Boker's bitters
twist of lemon

Monty's Best

4 parts Hollands gin
1 part ginger liqueur
STIR

Night Cap

4 parts Hollands gin
2 dashes Angostura Bitters
2 dashes sugar syrup
STIR - lemon peel & pineapple slice

Silver Cocktail

2 parts French vermouth
2 parts Hollands gin
1 dash gum syrup
2 dashes orange bitters
2 dashes maraschino
STIR–lemon twist

Wachholderbeeren Hahnschwanz

4 parts Hollands gin
2 dashes Abbott's bitters
1 dash sugar syrup
STIR

Yachting Club Cocktail

6 parts Hollands gin
2 parts French vermouth
2 dashes gum syrup
2 dashes Peychaud's Bitters
1 dash absinthe
SHAKE

ORANGE GIN

Cliftonian

3 parts yellow gin
3 parts Grand Marnier
1 part orange gin
1 part Swedish punsch
SHAKE
(*Winner of London Cocktail
Competition* 1935 *by Bert Nutt*)

Comet

2 parts orange gin
2 parts Lillet Blanc
2 dashes maraschino
STIR

Get Together

5 parts orange gin
3 parts dry vermouth
2 parts orange juice
2 dashes absinthe
SHAKE

Golden Dawn

Equal parts:
yellow gin
Calvados
apricot brandy
orange gin
dash of grenadine
SHAKE

Jackson Cocktail

Equal parts:
orange gin
Dubonet
2 dashes orange bitters
STIR

Landing Strip

Equal parts:
orange gin
dry gin
brandy
SHAKE

Leap Year

5 parts dry gin
2 parts orange gin
2 parts dry vermouth
1 part lemon juice
SHAKE

Misty Morn

Equal parts:
orange gin
passion fruit juice
Drambuie
SHAKE

Moulin Rogue

3 parts orange gin
1 part apricot brandy
3 dashes grenadine
STIR

Orange Milk Fizz

3 parts orange gin
2 parts lemon gin
1 tsp sugar
4 parts milk
Top up with club soda

Roman's Scandal

4 parts orange gin
2 parts dry vermouth
1 part red vermouth
1 part kirsch
dash of aromatic bitters
STIR

Round the World

Equal parts:
yellow gin
brandy
dry vermouth
red vermouth
orange gin
dash of absinthe
SHAKE

LEMON GIN

Baronial

7 parts Lillet Blanc
3 parts lemon gin
2 dashes Angostura Bitters
2 dashes Cointreau
SHAKE

Betty Dighton's Mint

5 parts lemon gin
2 parts orange juice
1 part Campari
1 mint leaf
SHAKE

Bucalf

4 parts Canadian whisky
1 part passion fruit juice
1 part green crème de menthe
dash of lemon gin
STIR

Chinese Lady

2 parts lemon gin
1 part grapefruit juice
1 part Yellow Chartreuse
SHAKE

Gloucester Glory

Equal Parts:
apricot brandy
dry vermouth
lemon gin
lemon juice
orange juice
SHAKE

Pescara

Equal parts:
lemon gin
dry vermouth
Cerasella
SHAKE

Windsor Jubilee

2 parts lemon gin
1 part lemon juice
1 part Aurum (orange liqueur)
SHAKE

MINT GIN

May Day II

4 parts mint gin
2 parts crème de cacao
2 parts cream
SHAKE

Mint Gin Cocktail

2 parts mint gin
2 parts white port
1 part dry vermouth
STIR

Mint Gin Collins

2 parts mint gin
1 part lemon juice
SHAKE
Strain into a highball glass and top
up with club soda and ice.

Mint Maiden

4 parts mint gin
3 parts lemon juice
2 parts orange curaçao
egg whites
SHAKE

Moscow Green

Equal parts:
mint gin
coffee liqueur
whole milk
STIR

Royal Mint

4 parts brandy
1 part mint gin
2 dashes Angostura Bitters
STIR

APPLE GIN

Apple Gin Toddy

2 parts sweet apple gin
1 part lemon juice
4 parts boiling water
2 dashes of aromatic bitters
STIR

Apple Martinez

2 parts dry apple gin
1 part red vermouth
2 dashes orange bitters
2 dashes maraschino
SHAKE

Coronation Café Royal
(Invented by W.J. Tarling)

3 parts sweet apple gin
1 part orgeat syrup
1 part kirsch
1 part lemon juice
dash of egg white
SHAKE

Ivy

(Created by T.E. Pooley)

Equal parts:
dry apple gin
yellow gin
Grand Marnier
dry vermouth
blue curaçao
lemon juice
SHAKE

Marigold

Equal parts:
dry apple gin
French vermouth
Calvados
SHAKE

Trapeze

4 parts sweet apple gin
2 parts lemon juice
3 dashes Abbott's bitters
STIR

MAPLE GIN

Taken from the Buffalo Distilling Company of the Pan American Exposition Booklet circa 1901.

Gin Fizz

6 parts maple gin
1 parts lemon juice
1 tsp sugar syrup
SHAKE–Top up with club soda.

Gin Rickey

4 parts maple gin
1 part lime juice
10 parts club soda

Gin Sangaree

6 parts maple gin
1 part sugar syrup
SHAKE
Strain into a small glass and add a dash of port wine and a sprinkle of nutmeg.

Martinez

Equal parts:
maple gin
red vermouth
3 dashes orange bitters
STIR

Silver Fizz

8 parts maple gin
2 parts cream
1 parts lemon juice
1 egg white
2 tsp sugar syrup
SHAKE– top up with club soda

(For a Golden Fizz use the egg yolk instead of egg white)

CRÈME YVETTE

Angel's Dream

Equal Parts:
Crème Yvette
maraschino
whipped cream
Layer in a liqueur glass.

Baby Titty

1 part anisette
1 part Crème Yvette
1 part whipped cream
Layer in a liqueur glass
and top with cherry.

Belmont

7 parts dry gin
1 part Crème Yvette
1 part St. Germaine Elderflower
2 parts lemon juice
Top up with soda water.

Blue Moon I

2 parts dry gin
1 part French vermouth
1 dash orange bitters
1 dash Crème Yvette
STIR
Strain and top off with claret.

Blue Moon II

4 parts dry gin
1 part Crème Yvette
STIR–lemon twist

Crow's Peck

2 parts yellow gin
2 parts Swedish punsch
1 part Van der Hum
1 part Crème Yvette
3 dashes peach bitters
STIR–orange twist

The Defender

6 parts Old Tom gin
6 parts sweet vermouth
1 part Crème Yvette
dash orange bitters
STIR

Eagle's Dream Cocktail

4 parts dry gin
1 part Crème Yvette
2 parts lemon juice
1 tsp sugar syrup
SHAKE

Lavender Lady

4 parts dry gin
2 parts calvados
2 parts Cointreau
1 part lemon gin
1 part Crème Yvette
SHAKE

Little Tickle

2 parts dry gin
1 part Crème Yvette
1 part vodka
SHAKE

London Pride

2 parts dry gin
1 part Crème Yvette
1 part passion fruit juice
SHAKE

NY Flyer

4 parts rye whiskey
2 parts lemon juice
1 part Crème Yvette
1 part maraschino
SHAKE

Perpetual Cocktail

1 part Italian Vermouth
1 part French vermouth
2 dashes crème de cacao
4 dashes Crème Yvette
SHAKE

Ping-Pong Cocktail

1 part Crème Yvette
1 part sloe gin
1 tsp lemon juice
SHAKE

Ruban Bleu

8 parts white rum
1 part Crème Yvette
4 parts lemon juice
ice
SHAKE

Stratosphere

1 part Crème Yvette
5 parts champagne
Add Yvette to champagne flute and
top up with champagne.

Union Jack Cocktail

2 parts dry gin
1 part Crème Yvette
SHAKE

Yvette's Rainbow

Layer a bar spoon of the following:
Calvados
Benedictine
Galliano
Green Chatreuse
white crème de cacao
maraschino
Créme Yvette

CRÈME DE ROSE

Alexandretta

3 parts dry gin
2 parts crème de rose
2 part fresh cream
SHAKE

Clayton's Cocktail

3 parts dry gin
1 part crème de rose
2 parts lemon juice
8 parts champagne
3 dashes orange bitters

Crescent Moon

1 part dry gin
1 part crème de rose
1 part lemon juice
Add ice to a highball glass
and top up with club soda.

The Eyfords

8 parts dry vermouth
1 part crème de rose
2 dashes of Boker's bitters
STIR

Happy Thought

Equal parts:
crème de rose
crème de violette
anisette
white crème de cacao
hite crème de menthe
cognac
SHAKE

Helen's Rose

6 parts white rum
4 parts crème de rose
3 parts lime juice
SHAKE

Lillian Russell

Equal parts:
crème de rose
crème de violette
Cream

Nonbillay

2 parts dry gin
2 parts red vermouth
2 parts Campari
2 parts lemon juice
1 part crème de rose
SHAKE

Rose Martini

6 parts vodka
1 part crème de rose
SHAKE

Tigermoth

2 parts dry gin
1 part lemon juice
2 dashes maraschino
2 dashes crème de rose
SHAKE

Turkish Tea

3 parts vodka
3 parts white rum
3 part lemon juice
2 parts crème de rose
12 parts Coca Cola

Vicomte Cocktail

4 parts dry gin
3 parts crème de rose
3 parts dry vermouth
SHAKE

CRÈME DE THÉ

Assam

4 parts rye whiskey
2 parts red vermouth
1 part crème de thé
3 dashes of orange bitters
STIR

Dispur

4 parts dark rum
2 parts crème de thé
8 parts still lemonade

Dong Yang Dong Bai

4 parts brandy
2 parts crème de thé
3 dashes Abbott's bitters
STIR

Earl of Essex

4 parts dry gin
5 parts tonic water
1 part crème de thé
Add ingredients and ice to a brandy
baloon.
Twist of orange

English High Tea

1 part gin
1 part crème de thé
1 part lemon juice
4 parts soda water

Rosie

4 parts gin
1 part crème de thé
1 part triple sec
2 parts lemon juice
SHAKE

CRÈME DE VIOLETTE

Aviation Cocktail

2 parts dry gin
1 part lemon juice
2 dashes maraschino
2 dashes crème de violette
SHAKE

Angel's Wings

Use cordial glass.
Equal parts:
raspberry syrup
maraschino
crème de violette
Top with Cream and
decorate with a cherry.

Attention Cocktail

Equal parts:
crème de violette
French vermouth
absinthe
gin
STIR

Eagle's Dream

6 parts dry gin
2 parts crème de violette
2 parts lemon juice
½ tsp sugar syrup
1 egg white
SHAKE

Huntington Special

Juice 1 lime
½ bar spoon sugar
1 oz pineapple juice
½ oz crème de violette
1/5 jigger Jamaica rum
¾ jigger brandy
SHAKE

Pousse Café

In a pousse-café glass, build in equal
layers:
grenadine
maraschino
crème de violette
Green Chartreuse
brandy

Snowball Cocktail

6 parts fresh cream
3 parts gin
1 part crème de violette
1 part white crème de menthe
1 part Anisette
SHAKE

Violet Fizz

6 parts dry gin
2 parts crème de violette
4 parts lemon juice
1 tsp sugar
SHAKE
Strain into a tall glass
and top up with soda.

FORBIDDEN FRUIT

Adam & Eve Cocktail

Equal parts:
dry gin
cognac
Forbidden Fruit
dash of lemon juice
SHAKE

Bachelor's Downfall

2 parts Forbidden Fruit
1 part brandy
1 part Lillet
SHAKE

Beaux Arts Cocktail
(from the Bustanoby Bar)

3 parts byrrh wine
2 parts Forbidden Fruit
STIR –gold leaf flecks

Close Harmony

2 parts dry gin
1 part Forbidden Fruit
1 part white rum
4 dashes grenadine
4 dashes lemon juice
SHAKE

Cupid's Bow

Equal Parts:
Forbidden Fruit
dry gin
Aurum
passion fruit juice
SHAKE

Dante

4 parts dry gin
2 parts fresh lime juice
1 part Forbidden Fruit
1 part cherry brandy
SHAKE

Dorchester of London

1 part Bacardi Rum
1 part Forbidden Fruit
2 parts dry gin
STIR–lemon twist

Dusky Maiden

2 parts Canadian whisky
1 part Forbidden Fruit
dash of egg white
2 dashes Angostura Bitters
SHAKE

Forbidden Fruit

Equal parts:
Forbidden Fruit
dry gin
white crème de menthe
SHAKE

Gift of the Gods

Equal parts:
Forbidden Fruit
dry gin
dry vermouth
STIR

Girl Pat

4 parts Canadian whisky
3 parts Forbidden Fruit
1 part lemon juice
2 dashes Angostura Bitters
SHAKE

Hell's Fire

5 parts yellow gin
2 parts Forbidden Fruit
2 parts lemon juice
1 part grenadine
dash of maraschino
SHAKE

Kick in the Pants

3 parts Rum
2 parts Forbidden Fruit
1 part lime juice
3 dashes Angostura Bitters
SHAKE

King's Bouquet '37

4 parts dry gin
3 parts Dubonnet Red
2 parts Forbidden Fruit
1 part lemon barley water
SHAKE
Prepare glasses with 4 dashes
Crème Yvette and then pour in
the mixed drink.

Nahlin

5 parts dry gin
3 parts dry vermouth
1 part apricot brandy
1 part Forbidden Fruit
SHAKE

Optimist

4 parts Canadian whisky
3 parts Lillet Blanc
1 part Forbidden Fruit
1 part Swedish punsch
1 part orange juice
SHAKE

Orchid

4 parts dry gin
2 parts lemon juice
2 parts pink crème de noyau
1 part Forbidden Fruit
1 part Crème Yvette
SHAKE

Prince Edward

Equal parts:
dry gin
Forbidden Fruit
Calvaos
Lillet Blanc
dash of grenadine
STIR–orange twist

Scots Gray

5 parts Lillet Blanc
4 parts Drambuie
1 part Forbidden Fruit
2 dashes lemon juice
STIR

Rose Marie

7 parts yellow gin
1 part vodka
1 part crème de noyau
1 part Forbidden Fruit
STIR

Rye Martini
(Invented by Toni Watkins)

Equal parts:
rye whiskey
dry vermouth
Forbidden Fruit
dash of absinthe
SHAKE

Tantalus
*(Recipe by Jack Bushby,
Cecil Bar, Paris)*

Equal parts:
Forbidden Fruit
brandy
lemon juice

The Zazz

2 parts Canadian whisky
2 parts dry vermouth
1 part Forbidden Fruit
1 part lemon juice
SHAKE

PIMENTO DRAM

Almost Rye

5 parts bourbon whiskey
1 part pimento dram
STIR–lemon twist

Balm Cocktail

8 parts dry sherry (Fino)
1 part Cointreau
1 part pimento dram
2 dash orange bitters
STIR

Lion's Tail

4 parts bourbon
1 part pimento dram
1 part lime juice
1 tsp gum syrup
2 dashes Angostura Bitters
SHAKE

King Edward

4 parts dry gin
2 parts Grand Marnier
1 part Swedish punsch
1 part pimento dram
SHAKE–lemon twist

Mexicano

4 parts white rum
3 parts kummel
3 parts orange juice
1 dash pimento dram
SHAKE

None But The Brave Cocktail

6 parts brandy
2 parts pimento dram
1 part lemon juice
1 part rum
2 dashes sugar syrup
SHAKE

FRUIT CUPS

Abel Green Summer Drink

1 part Pimm's No.1 Cup
1 part red vermouth
1 part Rhine wine
6 parts ginger ale

Blue Mountain Punch

4 parts rum fruit cup
3 parts lime juice
1 part pimento dram
8 parts ginger beer

Cairo Rail Bridge

4 parts rye fruit cup
4 parts lemon juice
2 dashes Abbott's bitters
2 dashes gum syrup
STIR

Casa del Fuego

4 parts tequila fruit cup
2 parts lime juice
dash of curaçao
SHAKE

Old Hall

5 parts dry gin
3 parts dry vermouth
1 part Pimm's No.1 Cup
1 part lime juice
SHAKE

Queen of Cups

1 part dry gin
1 part Campari
1 part gin fruit cup
2 dashes acid phosphate
STIR–twist of grapefruit peel

BOKER'S BITTERS

East India Cocktail

4 parts brandy
1 tsp curaçao
1 tsp pineapple syrup
3 dashes of Boker's bitters
2 dashes maraschino
STIR

Harvard

3 parts brandy
2 dashes Boker's bitters
SHAKE–lemon twist

Irish Cocktail

*This is a very palatable drink that was
noted as being a favorite of the Irish
members of parliament.*
3 parts Irish whiskey
2 dashes Boker's bitters
6 parts dry ginger ale

Japanese

3 parts brandy
1 part orgeat syrup
2 dashes Boker's bitters
STIR

Morning Cocktail

4 parts brandy
4 parts whiskey
3 dashes syrup
2 dashes curaçao
2 dashes Boker's bitters
1 dash absinthe
STIR–top up with club soda.

Soda Cocktail
(Non-alcoholic)

Take 1 bar spoonful sugar
2 dashes Boker's bitters
3 lumps of ice
1 bottle of plain or lemon soda
Serve in glass with spoon.

ABBOTT'S BITTERS
Arnuads Atomic Bomb

1 part gin
1 part bourbon
1 part red vermouth
2 dashes Abbott's bitters
SHAKE

Full house

1 part apple whisky
1 part Benedictine
1 part Yellow Chartreuse
1 dash Abbott's bitters
Serve frappe.

Manhattan

2 parts rye whiskey
1 part red vermouth
2 dashes Abbott's bitters
STIR

Peacock Gallery

4 parts cognac
2 dashes Abbott's bitters
1 dash absinthe
Serve frappe.

Swan Cocktail

4 parts lime juice
2 parts dry gin
3 parts dry vermouth
1 part pastis
2 dashes Abbott's bitters
SHAKE

Waldorf

1 part American whisky
1 part red vermouth
1 part absinthe
Dash Abbott's bitters
Serve frappe.

CELERY BITTERS

Bloody Mary

4 parts vodka
5 parts tomato juice
2 parts lime juice
3 dashes celery bitters
2 dashes Worcester sauce
STIR

Celery Gin & Tonic

2 parts gin
2 parts tonic water
2-3 dashes of celery bitters

Fourth Regiment
from Commander Livesey

2 parts rye whiskey
1 part red vermouth
2 dashes each of celery, orange
and Agostura Bitters
STIR–lime twist

Linnaeus

4 parts dry gin
1 part red vermouth
1 part dry vermouth
2 dashes celery bitters
SHAKE

Isthmus Cocktail

3 parts mezcal
3 parts lime juice
2 dashes celery bitters
SHAKE

Red Snapper

4 parts dry gin
5 parts tomato juice
2 parts lime juice
3 dashes celery bitters
STIR

KHOOSH BITTERS

Marion #1

Equal parts:
brandy
Grand Marnie
dry vermouth
2 dashes Khoosh Bitters
STIR

Monkey Island

2 parts dry vermouth
1 part dry gin
1 part sloe gin
2 dashes Khoosh Bitters
SHAKE

HERCULES

Angler Cocktail

6 parts dry gin
2 parts Hercules
2 dashes Angostura Bitters
2 dashes orange bitters
SHAKE–lemon twist

Bullfighter

2 parts tequila
1 part Hercules
1 part Grand Marnier
SHAKE

Ramon

6 parts dry gin
2 parts Hercules
2 parts dry vermouth

Zed Cocktail

Equal parts:
Hercules
apple brandy
SHAKE–lemon twist

GROSIELLE SYRUP

Celebration

2 parts daiquiri rum
2 parts fresh grapefruit juice
1 part gin
1 part grosielle syrup
SHAKE

Eton Blazer

4 parts dry gin
4 parts lemon juice
2 parts grosielle syrup
2 parts kirsch
STIR - top up with club soda.

L'Avenir

Equal parts:
grosielle syrup
apple syrup
raspberry syrup
1 egg
SHAKE

Nineteen Twenty Cocktail

6 parts dry gin
2 parts dry vermouth
2 parts kirsch
1 dash grosielle syrup
1 part orange bitters
STIR

Strawberry Vermouth

5 parts dry vermouth
1 parts gin
2 tsp grosielle syrup
STIR–halve fresh strawberries; top
up with lemon-lime soda.

OTHER FLAVORED SPIRITS

French Kick

4 parts yellow gin
2 parts dry vermouth
2 parts kirsch
1 part strawberry brandy
SHAKE

Tulane

Equal parts:
dry gin
French vermouth
strawberry brandy
SHAKE

The Hobo

3 parts Canadian whisky
2 parts Lillet Blanc
1 part cherry whisky
STIR–orange twist

ORANGE GIN

A simple process of infusion makes orange gin. A suggested recipe is given below:

1 liter dry gin
15g orange peel (no pith)
Approx. 65g sugar

Infuse the orange peel in the gin in a sealed container, tasting every few days to check its flavor profile. When a suitable intensity of flavor has been reached (around two weeks), remove the peel and fine-strain the liquid. Allow the spirit to rest for a week before adding sugar to taste and shaking until all sugar is dissolved. Bottle and allow to mellow in the bottle for four weeks before consumption.

An alternative method is to mix 400g of orange marmalade with 1 liter of dry gin. Allow two weeks for the marmalade to completely dissolve. Fine-strain, bottle and allow 2-4 weeks for the spirit to mellow.

LEMON GIN

A simple process of infusion also makes lemon gin:

1 liter dry gin
15g lemon peel (no pith)
2g cracked green cardamom pods (optional)
Approx. 65g sugar

Infuse the lemon peel and cardamom in the gin in a sealed container, tasting every few days to check its flavor profile. When a suitable intensity of flavor has been reached (around two weeks), remove the peel and fine-strain the liquid. Allow the spirit to rest for a week before adding sugar to taste and shaking until all sugar is dissolved. Bottle and allow to mellow in the bottle for four weeks before consumption.

MINT GIN

As there are currently no mint gins in production, here are some recipe ideas for making some in-house. The simple way to make mint gin is to use dried mint leaves, such as those found in mint tea bags. It is important to check the ingredients to ensure they contain 100% mint leaf. Once the tea has infused, strain and sweeten it.

Peppermint Tea

1 liter dry gin
12 g peppermint
33 g sugar

Sweet flavor with a bold, straightforward character that is very mixable.

Mixed Mint Tea

1 liter dry gin
14g mint tea (blend of peppermint, spearmint and field mint)
33g sugar

This has a menthol nose with some vanilla and butter. The peppermint is at the start of the flavor, followed by the juniper and coriander of the gin and then crisp spearmint and menthol on the finish.

APPLE GIN

1 liter dry gin
33g apple flesh (no peels, cores or seeds)
sugar to taste (for sweet apple gin only)

Infuse the apple flesh in the gin in a sealed container, tasting every few days to check its flavor profile. When a suitable intensity of flavor has been achieved (around four weeks), remove the apple and fine-strain the liquid.

To make dry apple gin, bottle the liquid and allow it to mellow in the bottle for around eight weeks before consumption. To make sweet apple gin, allow the spirit to rest for a week before blending in sugar to taste. Bottle the gin and allow to mellow for around eight weeks before consumption.

GENERIC FLAVORED GIN

In addition to these specific recipes, there are myriad of other ingredients that can be used to make flavored gins, some with more historical precedence than others. It would be impossible to cover all of these so, instead, here is some general advice that will hopefully help you to experiment.

The main method of flavoring gin, or indeed any spirit, is to use infusion; this is as true today as it was 200 years ago. This typically involves steeping the ingredients in the spirit and allowing the spirit to absorb the flavor. The higher the ABV of the alcohol, the quicker the rate of flavor extraction. During the infusion process, it is best to store the spirit in a clean, sealed container made of either glass or stainless steel.

It is recommended that you then taste it every few days so that you can monitor the intensity of flavor and bottle when the desired intensity has been reached. At this point, you will need to strain the liquid, using both a fine sieve and muslin cloth or coffee filter to remove the raw ingredients and any sediment. You can then add sugar to taste, dilute your spirit to your desired strength, and bottle.

FORBIDDEN FRUIT

1 liter aged grape brandy
17g orange peel
17g pink grapefruit peel
100ml honey

Infuse the citrus peels in the brandy in a sealed container, tasting every few days to check on the flavor profile. When a suitable intensity of flavor has been reached (around two to four weeks), remove the peel and fine-strain the liquid. Blend in the honey to sweeten as required and allow the flavors to marry for about a month before bottling.

CRÈME DE ROSE

Crème de rose is described in T. E. Carling's *Complete Book of Drink* as being made from essence of rose with hints of vanilla and citrus. A relatively neutral spirit base was common. However, in Charles H. Baker's *The Gentleman's Companion*, he describes making a rose liqueur brandy by using the perfect petals of eight big, red roses and infusing them for a month in cognac before blending with homemade rose petal syrup. This recipe is inspired by the T. E. Carling description:

1 liter vodka (barley-based is preferable)
14 drops rose essence
6 drops vanilla essence
2 drops lemon essence
2 drops orange essence
75g sugar

Although it is possible to use a neutral spirit base, a barley base adds a creamy texture and character to the finished product. Blend the vodka and the essence together and then add the sugar. Allow the flavors to marry together for two weeks before bottling.

CRÈME DE THÉ

1 liter neutral spirit
8g black tea leaves (i.e. Assam tea)
75g sugar

Place the tea leaves in a large muslin sack to allow easy infusion and, later, straining. Infuse the tea in the spirit for 20-30 minutes; the brewing time will vary depending upon the blend of tea used, so it is important to taste the spirit every five minutes or so to ensure the flavors do not become stewed and bitter. When you are happy with the flavor intensity of the liquid, remove the tea, fine-strain and blend in the sugar. Allow the flavors to marry for two weeks and then bottle.

CRÈME DE GENIÈVE

To make crème de genieve, mature juniper-only distillate, i.e. gin where juniper is its only botanical, in wood, either in a barrel or using staves, until a golden yellow color is achieved. Blend in sugar to taste; a recommended ratio being approximately 1 part sugar to 3 parts aged spirit.

GINGERETTE

1 liter dry gin
30g crushed ripe white currants
3g lemon peel
50g bruised ginger
80g sugar

Add the lemon peel, white currants and ginger to the container, and then add the sugar and the gin. Allow the mixture to infuse, undisturbed, for two weeks; fine-strain and bottle.

COCONUT SCOTCH

1 liter Scotch whisky
20g coconut flesh

In a sealed container, infuse the coconut flesh in the Scotch, tasting every few days to check on its flavor profile. When a suitable intensity of flavor has been reached (around eight to ten weeks), remove the coconut and fine-strain the liquid. Sweeten as required and allow the flavors to marry for around a month before bottling.

CHERRY SCOTCH

1 liter Scotch whisky
20g pitted black cherries
1g fresh vanilla (optional)
Approximately 65g brown sugar

Infuse the pitted cherries and vanilla in the Scotch, in a sealed container, tasting every few days to check on the flavor profile. When a suitable intensity of flavor has been reached (around eight to ten weeks), remove the cherries and vanilla and fine-strain the liquid. Sweeten as required and allow the flavors to marry for a round one month before bottling.

APPLE WHISKEY

1 liter American whiskey
33g apple flesh (no peels, cores or seeds)
1g fresh vanilla (optional)
Approximately 50g brown sugar (for sweet apple whiskey only)

In a sealed container, infuse the apple flesh in the whiskey, tasting every few days to check on its flavor profile. When a suitable intensity of flavor has been achieved (around four weeks), remove the apple and fine-strain the liquid.

For dry apple whiskey, bottle and allow to mellow for eight weeks before consumption. For sweet apple whiskey, allow the spirit to rest for a week before blending in sugar to taste. Bottle and allow to mellow for eight weeks before consumption.

STRAWBERRY BRANDY

1 liter aged grape brandy
30g strawberries (without leaves)
Approximately 50g brown sugar

In a sealed container, infuse the strawberries in the brandy, tasting every few days to check on the flavor profile. When a suitable intensity of flavor has been reached (around four weeks), remove the strawberries and fine-strain the liquid. Allow the spirit to rest for a week before adding sugar to taste. Bottle and allow to mellow in the bottle for eight weeks before consumption.

RASPBERRY BRANDY

1 liter aged grape brandy
30g raspberries (without leaves)
Approximately 60g brown sugar

Infuse the raspberries in the brandy in a sealed container. Taste every few days to check on the flavor profile. When a suitable intensity of flavor has been reached (around four weeks), remove the raspberries and fine-strain the liquid. Allow the spirit to rest for a week before adding sugar to taste. Bottle and allow to mellow for eight weeks before consumption.

GROSIELLE SYRUP

3kg ripe red currants
boiling water
450g sugar for every 500ml of juice

Crush the fruit in a jar, and then stand the jar in a pan of boiling water and cook gently for two hours. Strain the liquid through a fine sieve and then add sugar to the proportion given above. Bring the mixture to a boil and cook for an added 15 minutes, removing any scum as it rises to the surface. Allow to cool before bottling.

RUM FRUIT CUP

This fruit cup takes inspiration from classic rum drinks and the flavors of 1950s Tiki culture. As such, it involves lime peel and a range of spices, including ginger.

1.2 liters dark rum
0.6 liters red vermouth
0.3 liters pimento dram
0.3 liters orange liqueur
15g lime peel
7g peeled ginger

Combine all of the ingredients and allow to macerate for at least one week. Each day, stir the mixture and taste to monitor its flavor. When you have achieved the desired flavor, fine-strain the mixture and, for the best results, allow an added four weeks for the flavors to marry together before bottling.

SCOTCH FRUIT CUP

This fruit cup takes inspiration from the Whisky Ginger and the Rob Roy cocktail. The ginger and orange give it a warming quality.

1.2 liters Scotch whisky
0.6 liters red vermouth
0.2 liters ginger wine / ginger liqueur
0.2 liters orange liqueur
0.2 liters maraschino
10g lemon peel
10g orange peel
15g cinnamon/cassia bark

Combine all of the ingredients and allow to macerate for at least one week. Each day, stir the mixture and taste to monitor its flavor. When you have achieved the desired flavor, fine-strain the mixture. For the best results, allow an added four weeks for the flavors to marry together before bottling.

VODKA FRUIT CUP

This fruit cup takes inspiration from the now defunct Vodka Pimm's.

1.75 liters vodka
0.75 liters ginger wine
0.6 liters orange liqueur
0.4 liters red vermouth
10g lemon peel
5g fennel seed

Combine all of the ingredients and allow to macerate for at least one week. Each day, stir the mixture and taste to monitor its flavor. When you have achieved the desired flavor, fine-strain the mixture. For the best results, allow an added four weeks for the flavors to marry together before bottling.

TEQUILA FRUIT CUP

This fruit cup takes inspiration from classic tequila drinks and is designed to be light and refreshing.

1.2 liters tequila blanco
0.6 liters red vermouth
0.6 liters orange liqueur
15g lime peel
10g cinnamon bark

Combine all of the ingredients and allow to macerate for at least one week. Each day, stir the mixture and taste to monitor its flavor. When you have achieved the desired, fine-strain the mixture. For the best results, allow an added four weeks for the flavors to marry together before bottling.

SOJU FRUIT CUP

This fruit cup takes inspiration from the flavors of South Korea–the home of the world's best-selling spirit, Soju–and where Green Tea and Persimmon are also popular flavors.

1.8 liters soju
50g green tea
0.8 liters red vermouth
0.4 liters orange liqueur
10g orange peel
15g persimmon flesh

Place the tea leaves in a large muslin sack to allow for easy infusion and, later, for straining. Infuse the tea in the spirit for 20-30 minutes; the brewing time will vary depending on the blend of tea used, so it is important to taste the spirit every five minutes to ensure that the flavors do not become stewed and bitter. When you are happy with the flavor intensity, remove the tea.

Add the vermouth, liqueur, orange peel and persimmon flesh to the tea-infused Soju and allow to macerate for at least one week. Each day, stir the mixture and taste to monitor its flavor. When you have achieved the desired flavor fine-strain the mixture. For the best results, allow an added four weeks for the flavors to marry together before bottling.

Further Reading

For updates to this book, check out www.craftofgin.com/book2.

ON~LINE RESOURCES

Cocktail DB   cocktaildb.com
Savoy Stomp   savoystomp.com
Summer Fruit Cup   summerfruitcup.com
Mixellany Limited: Free Online Library of Old Cocktail Books   mixellany.com/library.html

PRODUCERS OF SPIRITS AND LIQUEURS

Art of Drink   artofdrink.com
Bitter Truth   the-bitter-truth.com
Bob's Bitters   bobsbitters.com
Crème Yvette   cremeyvette.com
Citadelle Gin   citadellegin.com
Dr. Adam Elmegirab   bokersbitters.co.uk
FEW Spirits   fewspirits.com
Golden Moon Distillery   goldenmoondistillery.com
Haymans Gins   haymansgin.com
New York Distilling   nydistilling.com
San Francisco Bitter's Company   sanfranciscobitterscompany.com
Tempus Fugit   tempusfugitspirits.com

OTHER USEFUL BOOKS

Baker, Charles H. *Gentleman's Companion.* Eastford: Martino Fine Books. 2013
    ISBN-10: 1614273960.

Carling, T.E. *The Complete Book of Drink.* Aberdeen: Practical Press Ltd. 1951.

Conrad III, Barnaby. *Absinthe–History in a Bottle.* San Francisco: Chronicle Books. 1988.
    ISBN: 0-8118-1650-8.

Brown, J and Miller, A. *Spirituous Journey - A History of Drink–Book Two*. London: Mixellany Limited. 2009. ISBN: 978-1-907434-6-8.

Embury, David. *The Fine Art of Mixing Drinks*. New York: Doubleday & Company Inc. 1948.

Hallgarten, Peter A. *Spirits and Liqueurs*. London: Faber & Faber. 1979. ISBN 0-571-10114-3.

Haigh, Ted. *Vintage Spirits and Forgotten Cocktails*. Beverly: Quarry Books. 2009. ISBN: 1-59253-561-3.

Tarling, W.J. *Café Royal Cocktail Book*. Coronation Edition. Mixellany Limited. ISBN:0-9760937-5-8.

Saucier, Ted. *Bottoms Up*. New York: Greystone Press. 1951. ISBN: 978-1-891396-65-6.

Wondrich, David. **Imbibe**. New York: Penguin Group. 2007. ISBN: 978-0-399-53287-0.

INDEX

THE BITTER TRUTH

ESTABLISHED 2006

21ST CENTURY PRODUCERS of 18TH & 19TH CENTURY PRODUCTS

SPIRITS & LIQUEURS

Pink Gin & Sloe Gin

Pimento Dram

Apricot, Violet & Elderflower Liqueurs

Golden Falernum

Bitter Truth Elixir

BITTERS

Aromatic	Peach
Lemon	Celery
Orange	Chocolate
Grapefruit	Creole
Tonic Water	Jerry Thomas Decanter

THE SPIRIT OF HISTORY

TEMPUS FUGIT SPIRITS

Re-creators of Long-Lost Absinthes, Bitters, Spirits & Liqueurs

CRÈME DE CACAO

LIQUEUR DE VIOLETTES

GRAN CLASSICA BITTER

CRÈME DE MENTHE GLACIALE

FERNET DEL FRA E ANGELCO

KINA L'AVION D'OR

VOYAGER DRY GIN

As well as a Selection of
Verte & Blanc Absinthe.

Producers of Authentic Abbott's Bitters!

CALIFORNIA, USA

Dr Adam Elmegirab

Creator of Fine Bitters
Established 2009

BOKER'S BITTERS

SPANISH BITTERS

APHRODITE BITTERS

TEAPOT BITTERS
Also producing:
DR. HEATHER DUNCAN'S - SEASONAL CHRISTMAS BITTERS

Golden Moon Distillery
Maison de la Vie Ltd.
Distiller of Quality Spirits and Liqueurs

REDUX ABSINTHE SUPÉRIEURE
AMER DIT PICON (78 PROOF)
CREME DE VIOLETTA
DRY CURACAO
GOLDEN MOON GIN
COLORADO APPLEJACK
COLORADO GRAPPA

Golden, Colorado, USA

Premium Bitters Producer
Established 2008

CELERY BITTERS	CARDAMOM BITTERS
LIME BITTERS	CHOCOLATEBITTERS
GRAPEFRUITBITTERS	LAVENDER BITTERS
ORANGE BITTERS	AROMATIC BITTERS

SEATTLE, WASHINGTON, USA

SAN FRANCISCO BITTERS COMPANY

From the Cocktail Route of 1890s San Francisco

America's Largest selection of forgotten Bitters

RECEPTION	JAMAICAN GINGER	ALPINE
BOKER'S	BONNEKAMP	YERBA BUENA
SEGALAS	DAMIANA	PERUVIAN
KHOOSH	FLOWER DRUM	STOUGHTON

California, USA.

Lightning Source UK Ltd.
Milton Keynes UK
UKOW07f0719220515

252094UK00005B/71/P